Jacob Serenus Hartzell

Sin and Our Saviour

Forty serious sermons for forty serious days

Jacob Serenus Hartzell

Sin and Our Saviour
Forty serious sermons for forty serious days

ISBN/EAN: 9783337314613

Printed in Europe, USA, Canada, Australia, Japan

Cover: Foto ©Lupo / pixelio.de

More available books at **www.hansebooks.com**

Sin and Our Saviour

Forty Serious Sermons

FOR

Forty Serious Days.

By Rev. J. S. Hartzell, M. A.

Milwaukee, Wis.
The Young Churchman Co.
1895.

Contents.

Ash Wednesday. "Sanctify a Fast."	7
Second Day of Lent. "Where Art Thou?"	12
Third Day of Lent. Sin.	17
Fourth Day of Lent. Original Sin, Sins of Omission and Commission.	23

First Sunday in Lent.

Fifth Day of Lent. Sins of Habit.	29
Sixth Day of Lent. Sins of Character.	35
Seventh Day of Lent. The Besetting Sin.	41
Eighth Day of Lent. Sins which Crucify Christ.	47
Ninth Day of Lent. Death.	53
Tenth Day of Lent. Judgment.	60

Second Sunday in Lent.

Eleventh Day of Lent. Eternity.	66
Twelfth Day of Lent. Self-Examination.	73
Thirteenth Day of Lent. Repentance.	78
Fourteenth Day of Lent. Consciousness and Confession of Sins.	83
Fifteenth Day of Lent. Self-Consecration.	89
Sixteenth Day of Lent. "Son of David, have mercy on me!"	94

Third Sunday in Lent.

Seventeenth Day of Lent. "A Friend of Publicans and Sinners."	99
Eighteenth Day of Lent. Jesus the High Priest.	105

Nineteenth Day of Lent. Jesus the Good Shepherd. - - 110
Twentieth Day of Lent. Jesus at the Door. - - - 115
Twenty-first Day of Lent. Jesus the Water of Life. - - 121
Twenty-second Day of Lent. Jesus the True Vine. - - 126

Fourth Sunday in Lent.

Twenty-third Day of Lent. Jesus the Bread of Life. - - 131
Twenty-fourth Day of Lent. The Church. - - - 137
Twenty-fifth Day of Lent. Holy Baptism. - - - 145
Twenty-sixth Day of Lent. Examination and Eating. - 151
Twenty-seventh Day of Lent. "In Remembrance of Me." - 155
Twenty-eighth Day of Lent. In the Upper Chamber. - 161

Fifth Sunday in Lent.

Twenty-ninth Day of Lent. Gethsemane. - - - 167
Thirtieth Day of Lent. Watching with Christ. - - 173
Thirty-first Day of Lent. Betraying Christ. - - - 179
Thirty-second Day of Lent. The Denial. - - - 185
Thirty-third Day of Lent. The Mockery. - - - 190
Thirty-fourth Day of Lent. "Behold the Man." - - 196

Sixth Sunday in Lent.

Thirty-fifth Day of Lent. Carrying the Cross. - - - 201
Thirty-sixth Day of Lent. The Sorrow. - - - - 207
Thirty-seventh Day of Lent. The Desolation. - - - 213
MAUNDY THURSDAY. The Passion. - - - - - 218
GOOD FRIDAY. The Death. - - - - - - - 223
EASTER EVEN. In Paradise. - - - - - - 228

Preface.

THESE Lectures are a growth. They were delivered in different parishes and in successive years, each time with some additions and improvements. Some thoughts and materials were culled here and there, and woven into the fabric; and in such a way that at this day it is impossible for me to tell which is so gathered. This general acknowledgement is all I can make, except that I must state I am especially indebted to the Lent Manuals of Bishop W. W. How, Edersheim's Life of Christ, Manning's Sermons, Massilon's Conferences, A'Kempis' Imitation of Christ, Giles' Sufferings of Christ, DuBose's Soteriology of the New Testament, the Writings of the Apostolic Fathers, and to "Mercersburg Theology and Philosophy" which has furnished me with the groundwork of my dogmatic conceptions.

They are now published in obedience to the expressed wishes of many who heard the Lectures delivered; with the prayer that they may be blessed of God and a blessing to others.

J. S. HARTZELL,
Rector of Christ Church,
Mt. Pleasant, S. C.

The Rectory, May 4th, 1895.

Sin and Our Saviour.

ASH WEDNESDAY.

Sanctify a Fast.

Sanctify a Fast.—Joel ii. 15.

THE law of Moses, and the Sacred Year of the Jewish Church, prescribed numerous days and seasons of fasting and humiliation. But in times of distress or calamity, or in times of national disobedience and apostacy, special seasons of fasting were declared by the holy Prophets, that thereby the anger of God might be turned, and He repent Him of the evil and leave a blessing behind Him.

The great annual season of Fasting under "the Law and the Prophets" was "the time of the Passover," which commemorated the Day of Expiation. The Christian Church, adopting the idea from the Jewish Passover, preceded by its solemn season of fasting, celebrates the holy joys of Easter after a Forty Days of Lenten fasting.

What authority has the Christian Church for this? Our Saviour Christ nowhere prescribes fasting, one might say. No. But He more than prescribes it. As a Jew, and as One who was come to fulfil all the law and the prophets, He Himself kept all the fasts of the Jewish Ecclesiastical Year; and

He gave His disciples rules how they, the first fruits of the Christian Church, and the foundations on which that Church was built, should observe a fast. "When ye fast," said He, implying by His language that our Lord not only expected but took for granted that His disciples would fast.

He Himself faithfully kept all the fasts which His Father in Heaven had prescribed for His Jewish Church; and He gave His Apostles and Stewards of the Christian mysteries rules how they should fast. Thus it has come that the Christian Church has always observed seasons of fasting and prayer, and has disciplined her children by special abstinence, humiliation, and mortification of the body to prepare the spirit for the transcendent joys of Easter.

We are again within the threshold of this Great Fast, and the Epistle for this day—a day next to Good Friday the greatest Fast day in the Christian year—bids us "Sanctify a Fast;" while the Gospel warns us not to fast ostentatiously but humbly and in secret, ever mindful of the searching Eye of One who seeth in secret. Its story of sadness and suffering appeals to us most eloquently to do for Him, as far as human weakness can, what He has so mercifully done for us.

The question, then, for us all is, How shall we keep Lent?

It is a season especially appropriate for self-examination—for looking inwardly upon the heart and seriously, earnestly, prayerfully studying its character. We constantly confess to Almighty God that "we have left undone those things which we ought to have done, and have done those things which we ought not to have done"—but we never, perhaps, for a moment stop to consider what those omissions and commissions are which we confess, nor recount them with contrite sorrow and full purpose of amendment and new obedience. We confess, and that is all. We do not strive to overcome the evil or to amend the fault. Let us now look upon ourselves, sensible of God's displeasure for our sins, that, knowing our misdeeds we correct them, so "that the rest of our life hereafter may be pure and holy."

So also is it a season for self-denial. Pleasures and amusements, appetites and desires are all to be curtailed and disciplined—holding in subjection the body, suffering if needs be, so that the world may be brought to our feet and the soul rise above earthly thoughts and cares; not indeed as Christ did in the wilderness, for an abstinence that is beyond human endurance is not required of us; but rigid self-denial of all that is not consistent with the spirit of this Lenten season, self-denial of all that is not in harmony with the solemnities of these Forty Days, is required of God's faithful children. To bear the Cross of Christ is first to deny ourselves.

Every self-denial is a sacrifice. So the season of Lent demands that we should sacrifice, not only pleasures and desires of every sort, but ourselves as well. Indeed, "the mercies of God beseech us that we present our bodies a living sacrifice, holy, and acceptable unto God" at all times, but especially so in Lent, because it is the season that commemorates Christ's Sacrifice for our sins.

So is it a season of humiliation,—a season in which we humble ourselves before God, "acknowledging our wretchedness and lamenting our sins." While we no longer observe the ancient custom of putting on sackcloth and covering the head with ashes, still in spirit these customs must be observed. What we no longer show in dress and appearance we are still to feel in the heart. That self-abasement which we no longer manifest outwardly, we must still practice inwardly, "that we appear not unto men to fast, but unto our Father which is in secret, that our Father which seeth in secret, may reward us openly." Renouncing our sins which we lament, and condemning ourselves for committing those sins, we turn to the Lord our God "with all our heart, and with fasting and with weeping, and with mourning," rending our hearts and not our garments; then in the solemn hour we shall hear the sweet Voice from above speaking peace to our souls, and by divine grace we shall receive from God the new and contrite hearts which we pray for.

Thus, with Christ, our Example, we go into retirement for a while to be tempted, and thereby to learn obedience and gain a spiritual victory over the world without and the body within; and then come forth at the dawn of Easter, bringing the offering of a sanctified fast, and a victorious soul, and a submissive body. Throughout entire Lent we have Him, our Example, before our eyes. We follow Him in His Temptation, and remember "He was tempted like as we are yet without sin," and for our sakes overcame. We accompany Him in His sufferings, and remember that those sufferings were endured for us. Doing good and preaching the Gospel of the new Kingdom, yet tempted, despised, rejected, the judgment hall, the mockery, the thorns, the Cross come to view, and a sorrowing, sighing, bleeding, dying Saviour—our sins, our Saviour. With all this before our eyes we enter Lent with the determination, by self-examination and discipline to become more Christ-like, following in His footsteps, learning more of Him, doing more of His will, loving Him more, and thus, step by step, becoming more like Him in meekness, purity, obedience and holiness.

But alas! alas! O Lord, mayest Thou not say to some of us: "Why call ye me Lord, Lord, and do not the things which I say?" We should, therefore, in all our Lenten discipline, have the one thought and desire of worshipping God more sincerely, and of increasing our devotion to Him. We should aim, by a more rigid discipline of the body, to serve God more faithfully in spirit,—not, however, at the end of this dear season of Lent to return to the world with re-enforced and redoubled energies to hold high carnival with the pleasures which are but for a time; but that by a fast of the body in things earthly, we may enjoy a feast of the soul in things heavenly; that by a fast of the flesh in things carnal and worldly, we may have a feast of the spirit in things spiritual and eternal,—a bodily fast and a spiritual feast, which will carry their benefits into the other seasons of the Church year, and prove by our better life hereafter that this Lent has been well kept, and the humble prayer of the penitent heart, "Make me a clean heart, O God, and renew a right spirit within me," has been truly answered.

SECOND DAY OF LENT.

WHERE ART THOU?

And the Lord God called unto Adam, and said unto him, Where art thou!—Genesis iii. 9.

ADAM had been made in God's image and likeness, and for God's pleasure and delight. He walked with God; he talked with God; he communed with God in happy speech out of a loving heart. God loved the man He had made; Adam loved God. There was a devoted fellowship between them; an intercourse and communion next only to that between the angels and their God. Adam not only lived for, but lived in, his Creator; and, in return, God poured into Adam's mouth unnumbered blessings, and into his heart unbounded love.

But, alas! when God called, all was changed. There lay a cloud upon Adam's heart, and upon God's. Instead of walking boldly out to "seek after God, if haply he may find Him," he shrinks from God, and slinks away, hiding himself, as he supposed, among the leaves and bushes. Why this conduct? What has Adam done? "I was afraid, and hid myself," said he. Why afraid of God, who is all love and tenderness and sweetness? Why hide from Him whose presence is not only paradise but heaven? Why that feeling of fear and shame—why that sense of guilt and feeling of remorse and anguish of soul, which Adam showed by concealing himself from the sound of God's voice and the searching glance of God's eye? Had he forgotten that God is Omniscient, "who knoweth all things, and needeth not that any man should tell Him," "unto whom all hearts are open, all desires known, and from whom no secrets are hid?"

Yet, to him, in the cool of the day—not in ignorance, but in disappointment, in pity, in anger—came the penetrating cry: "Where art thou?"—thou, whom I made in My own image, and for My glory—thou, whom I trusted, and in whom I delighted—thou, upon whom I poured My best gifts, the blessings out of My hand and the love out of My heart—thou, whom I pronounced good, and whom I created for My fellowship—"Where art thou?" Out of the bushes comes the faltering, fear-smitten reply: "I was afraid, and I hid myself." It was the only answer he could give, and it betrayed the sin of his soul. "By one man sin entered into the world, and death by sin." "In Adam all die," and, in consequence, "the whole creation groaneth and travaileth in pain together until now." "Yea, the earth mourneth and fadeth away." "All the foundations of the earth are out of course." He became the slave of sin, the victim of sickness and bodily pain and anguish of heart, of evil temper and cruel lusts; and the unborn millions of his posterity the inheritors of his depraved, lapsed and apostate nature.

We all know the consequences of Adam's sin too well. It is not merely a matter of knowledge, but of daily experience. You and I are among those millions of inheritors of Adam's sinful nature and enslaved heart. You and I are his sons in sin as well as in the flesh. We carry the marred image and corrupted likeness of Adam in our hearts, and show it in our lives. We have sinned, we have sinned, we have grievously sinned against God, by thought, word, and deed. Not only to-day, and yesterday, and the day before, have we — you and I — done this evil and committed that offence, fallen into this temptation and into that sin, but our whole life — yours and mine — has been one of spiritual blindness and darkness and transgression and sin. "Behold, I was shapen in wickedness, and in sin hath my mother conceived me," was said by the Psalmist of us as of himself; and we are left "to eat the fruit of our way, and to be filled with our own devices."

To us, then, this question of God comes with equal force as it did to Adam; and we do well, on the threshold of this solemn season of Lent, to stop, and consider, and answer. To you and to me God calls, "Where art thou?" We reply, not that He may know, but that we may know; not to acquaint Him with our condition and our character, for He knows well — quite well — far too well; but to acquaint ourselves with it. What is our condition of mind and heart? What is our character before God — that God "who seeth in secret?" What are we doing for God, for the Church, for ourselves and our salvation — or not doing? How do we use all the privileges God gives us, and perform all the duties God lays upon us, and receive all the blessings God bestows upon us? Nay, more: as the principle of an evil lies deeper than the deed itself, so look searchingly into the depth of your heart — into the secret chambers of your soul, and there weigh God's question well, and see what answer you can give Him. What is your relation with God? What is the state of that heart which you once gave to God wholly to be His? How many evil spirits are lurking around it, or hiding within it? How many tempers and passions, how many desires and lusts, are seated there, and, with daily and hourly touch, are painting your heart—your character—with the "blackness of darkness"? What is the state of that soul which was once washed white in Divine blood, which was once dedicated as the temple of the Divine Spirit? Is it still wearing its ghostly whiteness, or is its beauty marred by the pollution of many sins? Is the Holy Spirit still abiding there and continuing His work of sanctification; or has He suffered daily and hourly interruptions by our transgressions, or, alas! been driven out by our persistent course in wilful sin? "Lo, Thou requirest truth in the inward parts," but "there is no faithfulness in our mouths, our inward parts are very wickedness." Sins, sins, sins—great and small—nothing but sins, are strewn along the whole path of our lives, and, alas! recorded in Heaven to our confusion and shame. If God should "hide His face from us, we would be like them that go down into the pit." If God would be extreme to mark what is done amiss, we could never abide it. "O Lord, rebuke me not in Thine indignation, neither chasten me in Thy displeasure. Have mercy upon me, O Lord, for I am weak;" "there is no health in my flesh because of Thy displeasure, neither is there any rest in my bones by reason of my sin." But Thou, Lord, "art a merciful God, full of compassion, long-suffering, and of great pity. Thou sparest when we deserve punishment, and in Thy wrath thinkest upon mercy."

Beloved, we have entered again the season of Lent. It is a season for repentance, and a season of grace. It is the voice of God saying to each of us: "Where art thou?" and bidding us turn from all evil and turn to our God. It is the voice of God bidding us to examine ourselves, to search our hearts, to try our souls, and to repent of the evil that is in us. It is the voice of God putting us to shame for our past failures, and offering His help and blessing and grace. "He hath searched us out and known us, and understandeth our thoughts long before." Then let us, this Lent, pray God to "strengthen our weak hands and to confirm our feeble knees," that this Lent may not be like other Lents, but be more earnest, more serious, more searching, and so more faithful and more full of good to ourselves and of blessing to others. Let the cry daily be on our lips: "Lord, save us; we perish;" and the prayer: "God, be merciful to me, a sinner." And then, when Easter dawns upon the world, our daily searchings and strivings ended, we can lift our hearts in faith and say: "Lord, now lettest Thou Thy servant depart in peace, according to Thy word; for mine eyes have seen Thy salvation."

THIRD DAY OF LENT.

Sin.

If we say that we have no sin, we deceive ourselves, and the truth is not in us.—I. John i. 8.

THERE is nothing more striking in the life of an individual, or in history, than the quick and vast transition in the life of our Saviour following His Baptism;—so quick in its descent from the glory of a kingdom, proclaimed and inaugurated, to a conflict with Satan; and so vast in its extent as to almost take from us the power to realize it. From the waters of Baptism to the wilderness, with its wild beasts; from the devout acknowledgement of the Baptist to the forsakenness and loneliness that followed; from the consecration and filial prayer of the Christ to the want and weakness of a Forty Days' Fast; from the descent of the Holy Ghost and the testimony of the voice from Heaven to the assaults of Satan;—what a contrast these were—what an antithesis! "He was led of the Spirit into the wilderness to be tempted of the devil." May we not say He was led by our sins to a conflict with the instigator of those sins, that He might conquer sin and Satan for us, and bring us the victory? Yea, what followed His Baptism was necessary to His work as Redeemer; and it was our sins—your sins and mine —that drove Him there, that tempted Him, that entered into a conflict with Him;—your sins and mine put Him to a severe and bitter trial, to a painful humiliation and an open shame. But for your sins and mine, and the sin of the whole world, He bore it all; and came forth from the conflict and from the wilderness, in very deed the Master His disciples afterwards called Him;—not only their Master, but the Master of Satan—the Lord and Master.

But, what is sin? We all know how to sin, though we may not be able to give the best definition of it. From our infancy we have sinned, though we then understood it not. Too well we know how to sin, and thus bring sorrow to the heart of our Saviour, and open anew the five wounds in His sacred Body, and crucify Him afresh. We know how to do it all; and we do it often, to our shame be it said. But do we know—have we ever thought—of the hatefulness, the heinousness, the sinfulness of sin? If we have thought of sin as affecting us, here and hereafter, have we ever thought what our sins must be to our Saviour, and to the dear Father in Heaven, whose love for our souls prompted Him to send our Saviour into the world that we might not perish in our sins, but be saved? Alas! that is an aspect we forget. We sin as if we alone were affected by it; forgetful of the sorrow and suffering it causes in our dear Saviour's breast and in our Heavenly Father's heart.

But let us see what sin is;—first, with reference to God's holiness. His nature is perfect in holiness and purity. Sin is the utter and absolute opposite. God is holy; we are—sin. God abhors that which is evil; with what feelings of pity and horror, then, must He look into the heart of sinful man and behold all the evil that lurks therein. We mar the beauty, and break the unity and harmony God has established everywhere in His universe. What is order we make disorder; what is law we make lawless. The pure we make impure; the lovely we cause to be at enmity with God. We insult the nature of God by our own transgressions and iniquities; and, as if that were not enough, we taint with the poison of evil in our hearts everything He has made. And God sees it all. "He hath set our misdeeds before Him; our secret sins in the light of His countenance." How hateful they must be—how hateful we must be—to Him who is of purer eyes than to behold evil, and cannot look on iniquity." We deserve to be spurned from His footstool, and to be crushed by His wrath. Yet, in His wrath He remembereth mercy; for, in spite of our vileness and hatefulness, "we have an Advocate with the Father," "and He is the propitiation for our sins, and not for ours only, but for the sins of the whole world."

So far with reference to God, who hates sin. Let us, secondly, think of sin with reference to him who instigates it—the Devil. He is God's personal enemy. Whatever God does, Satan strives to undo. It is he who goeth about sowing tares in the wheat. It is he that walketh about, like a roaring lion, seeking whom he may devour. Temptations and snares beset us on every side; and it is he—the Tempter—who sets them for our downfall and who is not far away. And not only he, but his host of evil spirits, like a vast army of evil-doers, are actively engaged in corrupting our souls and thwarting the will of

God in every instance. He furnishes the temptation and prompts the excuse for falling into it. He prompts the wicked thought, or word, or deed, which is treason against God and a betrayal of Christ; and offers the apology for our rebellion against our Divine Master. Hence the sinfulness of sin, as a rebellion against our God, and an obedience to His and our great enemy, the Devil.

But we have still another aspect in which to think of sin,—not only as affecting God, nor as affecting Satan, but also as affecting us. Satan prompts it; God hates it; but we suffer the penalty for it—an awful penalty, a terrible penalty, for "the wages of sin is death,"—death not only of our bodies, which would be awful and terrible enough, but also of that other and deeper member of our being, the soul; and who of us dare face that? Seriously think of our sins as deserving punishment, and think of the punishment in store for us because of our sins; and who can longer live in sin and invite punishment? Who can longer live in disobedience and invite the penalty? Think of our sin as bearing, in the soul, a two-fold fruit,—as leaving us in guilt, each sin leaving us more guilty; and as a power over us, holding us in its firm grasp and leading us perforce to other, to more, to greater sins. Think of our guilt, and think of Him who will not hold us guiltless; and what must be His anguish, as He lays before His searching Eye our naked hearts, and there sees all! Or what His indignation against us as He beholds us passive under the power of sin, when He has offered us the help of His Holy Spirit to overcome sin, and the Blood of His Dear Son to wash away all the deep and numberless guilty stains! Or what His wrath, if, after having been washed clean in the Blood of the Lamb and having received the Holy Spirit into our hearts, we again wallow in the mire of sin and quench that Holy Spirit of God! Terrible will be the penalty for such conduct—awful the death, of body and soul, for such trifling with God's mercy. Well may we "turn unto the Lord our God, with all our heart, and with fasting, and with weeping, and with mourning," beseeching Him, who is "gracious and merciful, slow to anger and of great kindness," to "be favorable to His people," and to grant us "perfect remission and forgiveness."

Yet, it is not only our death, guilty and deserving though we be, that is the wage of sin; but it has accomplished the death of One who was guiltless and innocent. He who "cannot look on iniquity" yet "laid on Him the iniquity of us all." That great humiliation, that life of patient suffering, that agony in the garden, that sweat of Blood, that feeling of forsakenness and despair, the buffeting and hollow mockery, the cruel scourging and crown of sharp thorns, the gall and the vinegar, the piercing nails, the burning thirst, the groans and prayers, and the awful death agony—innocent of any crime or fault and endured wholly for us; this was the wage of sin. His was a righteous Soul, bowing beneath the weight of human sin—our sin; and bowing of His own will for our sake. His was a sinless Person, enduring the sense of the world's stupendous guilt, and suffering for the world's enormous sin—your sin and mine. That is the wage of sin; that is what sin has done. Shame —thrice shame—yea, eternal shame upon us for still giving Him grief and suffering by our faithlessness and unbelief, and our sins and shortcomings; and shame upon us if this Lent will not bring us to our knees in perfect penitence, and a full resolve to be more like our Saviour in innocence and purity; and if we do not seek pardon for the sins we have committed and the suffering we have caused Him, and ask a will to obey and a heart to love Him hereafter as He hath loved us until now.

FOURTH DAY OF LENT.

ORIGINAL SIN: SINS OF OMISSION AND SINS OF COMMISSION.

They are all gone aside, they are all together become filthy: there is none that doeth good, no, not one.—Psalms xiv. 3.

THE Psalmist describes the corruption of the natural man. He states both the totality and the universality of human corruption; that sin has not only passed upon all men, but through the entire man; that sin is malignant and epidemic.

Why sin came into the world, why man was permitted to fall, why God, in His wise Providence, gave Him power and freedom either to do good or evil, are questions far beyond man's understanding, and belong only to the hidden mysteries of God. After all our surmising, we must still say: We know not.

But we do know that sin is here, and that we are all sinners; perhaps, if we would only acknowledge it, the vilest of sinners. Let us look for a while to-day at this deep power called Original Sin, and then at our Sins of Omission and Sins of Commission.

"By one man sin entered into the world, and death by sin." "In Adam all die." Adam did not die as Adam, but as man; his fall was not the fall of an isolated being, but of mankind. He was the father of the human race; and in his fall contracted a nature corrupt and sinful, estranged from God, and guilty and condemned, which passes upon all the children of Adam—the corrupt inclination, the sinful character, of that nature with the nature itself. We inherit all; the guilt as well as the nature that is guilty—a proneness to all evil, a backwardness to all good; and, over all, God's wrath and condemnation. We are "born a child of wrath;" we were sinful before we ever committed any sin; we had an evil ground in the will before ever we were conscious of any evil act. The bitter waters of uncleanness from the fountain of Adam's sin deluged the soul before ever our hearts felt the warmth of earthly love, or our eyes opened to the brightness of earthly light. It came with the nature we receive from Adam.

"All the flood of beings to whom Adam has transmitted his nature are evil and sinful. The evil penetrates their moral fibre, their flesh and blood, their imagination and intelligence, their very conscience and spirit."[*] The evil of our nature is the source of all our evil thinking and willing; that inborn sin, which is a part of our carnal being, gives origin to all those acts of sin, whether of omission or of commission, that so befoul our stream of life. It is a fact, and it is a power—a power that grows as we grow; that tightens its hold on us as we taste more and more of the forbidden fruit; that tempts more and more cunningly as we may, perchance, find an inclination to resist it; that fills us with delight more and more as we submit to it. And soon there is rolled up a vast debt against our soul of actual sins—sins of omission and sins of commission, sins

---

[*] Mason: "Faith of the Gospel."

by neglect and sins by transgression, sins in thought, in word, and in deed—sins, countless sins, of every description.

Sins of Omission and Sins of Commission. Let us look at these for a moment. What do we mean by Sins of Omission? We know full well what Sins of Commission are; but many of us, perhaps, chance not to have so clear a conception of what the other sins are, and how deadly they are. We frequently confess ourselves to have "left undone those things which we ought to have done, and to have done those things which we ought not to have done;" yet, when we think upon our sins, we think only of actual transgressions—sins of commission—and seldom, many of us, perhaps, never, of the things we have left undone—the sins of omission.

Look at the Parable of the "Unprofitable Servant," and see whether there is not danger—serious danger—in sins of omission. "He did not waste his master's goods, like the steward in the other parable; he did not spend all his portion in riotous living, like the Prodigal Son; he was not ten thousand talents in debt, like the unmerciful servant."* He simply "went and digged in the earth, and hid his lord's money," and brought it back without having made good use of it—left undone that which he ought to have done; and for this—mark well the words—for this he was "cast into outer darkness, where there is weeping and gnashing of teeth." We have, therefore, to face the solemn truth that, at the Last Great Day, the things we leave undone—the sins of omission—

---

* Trench.

will condemn us as much as the things we do, or the sins of commission. The same Voice speaks the same lesson of solemn warning, also, in other parables. What does the Parable of the Fig Tree teach but the condemnation of unfruitfulness? What does the Parable of the Vine and the Branches teach but that, not every branch that beareth *bad* fruit, but every branch that beareth *not* fruit, shall be cut down and cast into the fire? What is it that condemns those of "all nations" who shall be gathered before the "Son of Man" in the Great Day?—is it that they have been thieves, murderers, blasphemers? No. But, "inasmuch as ye did it *not*." That is the great accusation against them, the crime of which they are guilty. And the last word we have of them is that "these shall go away into everlasting punishment." What they have omitted—neglected; what they did not do of all the many things they ought to have done, was the sin that sent them "into everlasting punishment."

Thousands upon thousands of souls that have been purchased by Christ's Blood have been lost—are daily lost—not because they have been transgressors of God's Law by open or secret act, but because they failed to act—"left undone" what was their bounden duty to do. Otherwise, they may have been faultless, of blameless life and exemplary conduct; but still, in God's eyes, they have been "unprofitable servants."

Then, on the other hand, think of the actual violations of God's Law. Think of the sins of commission that make still more desperate our chance of salvation; for, if what we fail to do sends the soul into "everlasting punishment," what must it be when our numberless violations, great and small, by word and by deed, are taken into the account? We have broken every commandment of God—if not in the letter, at least in the spirit. We have been guilty of hypocrisy and duplicity—serving Mammon more than we do God. We have been guilty of "evil concupiscence and covetousness, which is idolatry." We have been guilty of a vain use of God's Name, if not of blasphemy. We have neglected prayer, and failed to "assemble ourselves together" for God's worship, remaining at home when we might, and should, have gone to church. We have been guilty of undutifulness, pride, vain-glory, and self-conceit; of violence and cruelty, "hatred and malice;" of intemperance and gluttony in our thoughts and desires, as well as in eating and drinking; of some form or other of dishonesty in depriving another of that which was his due, whether of wealth, or influence, or character; of gossip and slander and equivocation; of envy and coveting. We are commanded to give of our substance as the Lord hath prospered us; but we do not. We are commanded to keep unspotted from the world this body that has, by Baptism, become the Temple of the Holy Ghost; but we do not. We are commanded to Sacramentally eat and drink of the Lord's Body and Blood, "in remembrance of Him;" but we leave God's house when that service begins, as if to say, "This I will not do." Thus, there is not a command—in the Decalogue or out of it—that we have not broken, in the spirit or in the letter. "We are all gone aside; we are all together become filthy; there is none that doeth good—no, not one." "All we, like sheep, have gone astray; we have turned every one to his own way," and "there is no health in us."

Let us take this seriously to heart this Lent. Think how we—you and I—have offended God numberless times in all these numberless ways; how we have caused Him grief and pain; how we have wounded His heart and pierced His soul, not only by our conduct at times, but by our whole past life; not only by our "going aside" and "becoming filthy," but by remaining away from Him and living in sin. If we do, this will be a well-kept Lent; and, when Easter comes, there will come with it a happier and a holier hope.

FIFTH DAY OF LENT.

Sins of Habit.

TO-DAY let us think about Sins of Habit. We know what terrible a thing sin is; let us see how much more terrible it is when it becomes a habit.

What is a habit? Anything that is done again and again,—that is done by repeated acts,—that is persisted in, becomes a habit. Each act of sin goes toward forming the habit of sin. And there is a power in habit, so that it masters us and we become a slave to habit; and if the habit be a sinful one, a slave to sin. Frequent repetition of anything makes it second nature to us. What was at first done rarely, and with conscientious scruples against doing it, will, by repetition, become a part of ourselves, destroying our sense of its wrong. It is a sin of habit—a sin that we have gradually fallen into.

You can best understand the power of habit, and the power of a sinful habit, when you reflect on drunkenness, or swearing, or lying, or sins of a similar character. You may not be guilty of any of these, but you come in contact with them in your daily life. You know their influence over others; you know their effect upon the character; and you know God's wrath against those who commit such sins. You know how displeased God must be to see His children consenting to the least temptation of Satan;

and how angry He must be if the consent is to a great evil. You know what effect drunkenness, for instance, has on a man's own life, and on those who have to live with him and depend on him.

But you are guilty of none of these great sins of habit—drunkenness, swearing, lying, and the like. I speak to Christian people, to whom they are hateful; who recoil from them, and abhor them in their inmost soul; who would be ashamed to be even sometimes found consenting to such sins, and more than ashamed to have such sins become a habit with them.

Yet there are sins, not so open, so glaring, so manifest, not so hurtful and hateful according to our notion, perhaps, but alike hateful to God; in which some of us sometimes indulge; into which persons who try to lead pure and holy lives sometimes fall. And they are sins of habit, too, notwithstanding that the grace of God is given them to resist and overcome. Because they are not transgressions of the weightier matters of the law, they seem small and unimportant to us; and yet, they are as deadly as the worst sins, gnawing at the soul's life with a slow and unnoticed, yet with a steady and sure, progress; and therefore to be all the more watched and guarded against because of the hidden and unsuspected evil.

But let us first see how sin develops. There are three stages. There is first the temptation. This is not yet sin; it is only the door through which we pass to sin. Were it sin, God would not tempt us, nor suffer us to be tempted; yet He tempts us, that, by the discipline of our minds and hearts, by a quick and firm effort of the will to overcome, and with the help of His grace given us with the temptation, we might grow in grace and in purity and holiness.

Next, after temptation, comes what is called delectation; a growing delight in, and desire for, that to which we are tempted. Here sin begins. This delight and desire we must instantly stop, by shutting our senses against it and taking our minds away from that which is tempting us. For, if we do not, it will pass into the third stage, which is consent, in which the sin is completed.

These are the stages through which we pass when we fall into great, or mortal, sin. Yet we follow the same course, in these sins of habit which we consider slight, but which are as full of evil and as harmful to Christian character as any other, because they lie at the very base, and eat their way into the soul at its very center.

Let us lay open our heart before us. Let us peer into its darkest recesses. Let us pass from chamber to chamber, from one dark corner to another, and uncover everything beneath which the very least of these sins of habit—that look to us so innocent—may lurk or hide. Let us spread our souls before us for conscientious self-examination, as they will one day be spread before the All-searching Eye of Him who seeth in secret; and see if there be any guilty stains upon them.

One of the commonest sins of habit, and one of the most dangerous because it is not considered a sin either by the world or by us, is sloth. I do not mean sloth in our every-day life, in our worldly affairs, in our business. One may be very active in these, and yet in that which should most concern him, which should be dearest of all to him—his spiritual acts and spiritual life—be very slothful. Let us suppose ourselves looking upon the average congregation in worship—our own will do very well. We find that not only the minds but the bodies of some are the victims of sloth. Our outward posture tells that we must kneel on comfortable cushions, or we cannot kneel at all. During prayers we have wandering thoughts and looks, an undevout mind, and are careless; and are called back to our devotions only by the feeble "Amens" from a half-dozen throats that seem to be so tired. Our responses are cold and indolent, with little heart or will. All through the service we give evidence that we hate to make an effort. And we think we are doing ourselves no harm, and that God whom we profess to worship cannot but be pleased. There is too much sloth in our worship, where there should be warmth and whole-heartedness.

Another sin of habit into which we all fall, because our depraved nature is almost unchecked there, is the indulgence of the imagination. Our thoughts take wings, and we fancy things we should not, and picture to ourselves things that are harmful and sinful. This is the case with great sins, which none of us would be guilty of; which we would not speak of, much less do; sins that are so plainly sinful that every good heart will shrink from them with pain and horror. All thoughts that are in any degree concerned with what is impure, immodest, unfit for a Christian to talk about or do, leave upon our mind and our character a taint of evil; and are also deeply hateful to Him who knoweth the very thoughts of man. But there are sins of the imagination that are less plainly sinful. For instance; we have had a difficulty, or a quarrel, with some one; and we go home thinking and brooding over it, and imagine ourselves still engaged in a heated dialogue, making the other person say what he did not and perhaps would not say, and giving reply. We thus aggravate the quarrel by making our anger more biting.

There is still another, and very common, sin of habit into which we fall—all of us; and yet which is forbidden by the Master and by His Apostle. It is that of censoriousness. We are too fond of thinking evil of our neighbor, in violation of that charity which "thinketh no evil," but "believeth all things" and "hopeth all things." We are too fond of dragging into the light of day the faults of others; and while we are doing this we "think of ourselves more highly than we ought to think." Who knows but that the other, with all the faults which we lay bare in him, is more a man after God's own heart than we are? Who knows that the other is not in God's sight better than we are who condemn him? Why shall we pass by our own faults, and pick at those of others, when, with the same temptations and the same training, we might have been no better than they? It is reasonable, it is charity, it is a Christian act, to think others better than ourselves; and it is a part of our Christian duty to consider ourselves that publican and sinner of the parable, who is unworthy to lift his eyes unto heaven.

There are other sins of habit—gluttony, lust, and

the like—which I need but name to remind you of their hatefulness and sinfulness.

May we this Lent shake off those sinful habits into which we may have fallen, and pray, by God's grace, they may abide with us no more.

SIXTH DAY OF LENT.

SINS OF CHARACTER.

SINS of character are more secret, more hidden, more subtle, and more dangerous than sins of habit. Sins of habit affect our character; but sins of character are at the base of our character and form our character. Sins of habit are like mud that we have splashed upon ourselves—indulgences in wickedness; sins of character are part of ourselves, of our natural disposition, innate qualities of our being. Sins of habit are what we think, or what we say, or what we do; sins of character, what we are. It is evident, then, that sins of character are more difficult to deal with, needing much knowledge of our inmost heart, and much grace and much humility, and needing much heart-searching and watchfulness, lest some of the more hidden sins of character escape our notice.

An ancient Oracle, when asked what is of all things the best, answered: "To know thyself." One of the English poets tells us that "The proper study of mankind is man." As sins of character are a part of ourselves let us for a while try to study and to know ourselves—at least our sins; and let us do this honestly and conscienciously. Let us look into our hearts determined to see ourselves as others see us. Let us throw the light into every nook and corner, that nothing may escape our search; and that we may see clearly what we are—what guilty inmates we harbor in that which is God's temple. Let us leave behind all self-love, and make the search in deep humility; for we shall not be long in finding out many sad truths about ourselves. And, while we are searching our hearts for our sins of character, let us think of all the precepts and commandments that each discovered sin has violated,—it will do us good, and will be a part of our Lenten discipline. Let us compare our lives and character with those pictured and described to us of holy men in the Bible; that the contrast may show us more clearly our faults and deformities. Above all, let us study our hearts in the light of that one Life that has been given us as our Pattern; that we may see how far short we come of that which He expects of us.

Let us do as we did before—look a few of the chief sins in the face; all the while examining ourselves to see whether we are guilty of them.

One of the most prominent of these sins of character—because one of the most common—is pride. It is a characteristic of this sin that we are unaware of it, or deny its existence; yet it is a fault with a great many. And often when we deny that we are proud, we are even too proud to confess that which we are. It is an abiding state of the heart, permeating one's whole being, entering into everything we say and everything we do. It crops out in our walk, our conduct, our speech. Yet it is not always in supposing one's self better than others. Pride may be found under a great deal of meekness and humility. It is not only the haughty that are proud; but the humble may be proud also. One may be too sensitive, too easily offended, or unduly anxious about the opinions of others about ourselves, or fancy slights where none are intended, or stand on rights or dignity. He considers himself only true to himself, and therefore sees no pride in his conduct; but to others, especially those who though innocent of wishing them any harm are affected by his conduct, the proud spirit is very apparent.

Another sin of character, equally common, is anger. How evil and sinful a thing this is many of us may know. How many other sins it leads to, we may all have sometime seen. How it tends to one of the greatest sins forbidden in the Decalogue, that of murder, we also know. Its tendency is always to do harm, or to wish evil, to another. But anger is sinful not alone because it leads ofttimes to murder, but because it has in its composition all the essentials of murder. In fact it is murder—not of the body but of that which is often dearer to a man than his body, that is, his good name and character. The use of hurtful or abusive words—the nursing in our hearts of any unkind or evil feelings, is murder of that which is of more value than the body. "Whosoever hateth his brother is a murderer." So speaks the Apostle; and he is only illustrating the doctrine of our Lord who teaches us that if any evil be in the heart it is as sinful as if it were in the deed.

Another sin of character is covetousness. This consists not only in desiring another man's property, but it has to do, also, with getting and spending our own; not only in wishing for our own that which is our neighbor's, but in the eagerness with which we take what is coming to us, and the tight grip we keep on it after we have it. For one can be covetous, and yet, for one reason or another, have no opportunity to show it in act; because it is a state of the soul. And one of the evils of covetousness is that we deny that we are such. We put our acts on other grounds—prudence, carefulness, economy, frugality, and the like; but we do not admit, nor suspect, that we are covetous, so subtle and secret is the snare of this sin. All the while we are dissatisfied with our lot or our station in life; we wish for a greater sphere and wider opportunities; we want more, and ever more, and other, and better, than we have. We are impatient; life becomes dull, and we become fretful. Our imagination pictures to us a glorious future, and we long for it. Our neighbor's success tells us of great possibilities, and we covet them—and, perhaps, are envious of our neighbor's success. Yet, it is not only in getting and spending money, or in the discontentment we show with our lot and our fortune in life, that we show our covetousness, but, also, in the spirit with which we support our religious and ecclesiastical obligations. It is that spirit shown by a very wealthy man who once paid seven hundred dollars for a private box at the theater and next Sunday put five cents into the plate in church. Do we give to the Church in proportion as God hath prospered us? Do we give with a willing heart? Questions like these are pertinent and timely during Lent. But, while we quicken our pace in the performance of our religious duties, let us not forget the wider sphere in which this sin may be shown, and both pluck up out of our hearts every trace of covetous desire and "set our affections on things above;" for we are taught not only that the Lord abhorreth the covetous, but that the covetous shall not inherit the kingdom of heaven (Ps. x. 3; I. Cor. vi. 10).

A fourth sin of character is selfishness. Who is not selfish? What heart, o'er all the earth, is not a selfish heart—perhaps not always, but, at least, sometimes. Selfishness is self-indulgence. Who is not fond of indulging himself? The miser and the spendthrift, the ill-tempered and the good-natured man, each in his own way, indulges himself, and in that indulgence shows one or another form of selfishness. Among the worst of the countless forms which this sin takes may be mentioned cold-heartedness, uncharitableness, and like states of feeling, in which we withdraw from others, and build around our hearts a Chinese wall through which neither love, nor sympathy, nor sense of duty, can effect a passage. We forget all about duty, and smother sympathy, and live in our little burrows regardless of the rest of the world. Our great Pattern here puts to shame our selfish lives. He lived solely for others; we live solely for self. He unselfed Himself, constantly doing acts of kindness to those who wished Him harm, and even forgiving and praying for those who nailed Him to the cross; we demand "an eye for an eye and a tooth for a tooth," and love our neighbor, but hate our enemy. If anywhere we discover this sin in our hearts, let us pray that "this mind which was in Him may also be in us;" that we may know less an less of self and more of God and God-likeness.

Of the many other sins of character, I will mention only one more—hypocrisy. This is appearing to be what we are not. It is in the sphere of morals what counterfeiting money is in business. It is assuming a character that does not belong to us. It is unreality. And this sin shows itself not only in our outward life and morals, but in religion, as if we thought we could deceive the Eye that is always upon us, "beholding the evil and the good."

Many more sins of character might be named—obstinacy, hardness of heart, worldliness, and the like. How they fasten themselves upon the soul! How they twine themselves around the heart! How natural they seem to us, because woven in the very texture of our character! Yet, we are to cast them off. We are to conquer these enemies. Strong as they seem to us, strong as Satan may be, God's "grace is sufficient for us." "Whensoever we call upon Him, then shall our enemies be put to flight."

SEVENTH DAY OF LENT.

THE BESETTING SIN.

Let us lay aside every weight, and the sin which doth so easily beset us.—Hebrews xii. 1.

IN the beautiful imagery of the Apostle, life is called a race. We are all contending for an "incorruptible crown," a "crown of life," more enduring than monuments, and that tells a victory greater than has ever been carved on stone.

Like all other races, this for the crown of life is circumscribed by conditions and beset with difficulties. Like all other races, to subscribe to the conditions may be a small task; to enter upon it may be comparatively easy; the beginning may be full of promises. But soon the weight we may be carrying may be too heavy; or the path may become thorny; or our feet may become entangled in weeds and briars; or the stones heaped up in the path may wound our feet and retard our progress. The morning is full of freshness, and the start well made; but the burden of the day is hard to bear; then come twilight, evening, night, darkness—disappointment and defeat.

So in the race for the "crown of life," of which the Apostle speaks. The fetters that bind and keep back the soul must first be gotten rid of; the burdens of many sins that now weigh down the soul must first be laid aside; all the snares and entanglements in our pathway, the thorns that are likely to prick our feet, the stones over which we are liable to fall, must either be cleared away or entirely avoided; especially the thorn that wounds us more sharply than all others—"the sin which doth so easily beset us," which hinders us at every step, must be plucked out and cast aside.

Let us think for awhile to-day of this principal thorn in our flesh—this besetting sin. It may differ in each of us. No two of us may be tempted or attacked by Satan with the same evil, or in the same way. Yet we each know our great weakness; the sin which has the most power over us; the temptation which is least resisted and overcome; the evil which most delights and enslaves us. We each know what it is by which we most often suffer defeats. Think of it in the depth of your heart. Untwine it from your heart, and bring it into the clear light of day. Look at it seriously; see it as God must see it, weighing well not only its power over you, but its guilt, in what it is both to yourself and to God, whom it greatly offends.

You and I have promised, in the most solemn way, and at a most solemn time—the time of our Baptism—to "renounce the devil and all his works, the vain pomp and glory of the world, with all covetous desires of the same, and the sinful desires of the flesh, so that we will not follow nor be led by them." You and I have promised, before God and His witnesses, to "renounce the world, the flesh, and the devil;" to resist all temptations that come from these sources; to "obediently keep God's holy will and commandments, and walk in the same all the days of our life." Yet we do not obediently keep His will and commandments, nor walk as "children of light." In one particular, at least, if not in many more, we are all transgressors of God's law.

A peculiarity of a besetting sin is, that it is often so hidden, so concealed, that we fail to recognize it as a sin. If we know it at all, it is only as a weakness of the flesh, or as a part—a characteristic—of our nature for which we do not hold ourselves responsible. We think God made us so;—He made us proud, or ill-tempered, or greedy;—He made us with strong desires and appetites and passions. But not so. These are but the ways in which original sin has developed in us; the medium through which the evil nature inherited from Adam makes itself felt. And, because we take them as inherent parts of our being, we fail to look on them as sins. Yet, we are to guard against these sinful developments of our nature, these temptations from within us, as much as we should, and must, guard against and overcome temptations from without.

But our besetting sin may be one of which we have long been aware. We have fought against it, perhaps, as well as we could, but it has taken such hold on us that it has, in a sense, become a part of our nature. Drunkenness, uncharitableness, deceitfulness, gambling, sloth, dishonesty—one of these, or one of the numberless other sins—may be our besetting sin; the one sin that has such hold on us that we scarce can do anything against it.

Or, the entire world, in the midst of which we live, may be one continued temptation. The different situations in life, the different circumstances which arise, may each unite with our natural corruption, for the purpose of weakening or seducing us. Wealth corrupts, poverty exasperates; prosperity exalts, affliction depresses; business preys upon us, ease renders us effeminate; knowledge inflates, ignorance leads us into error; pleasure seduces, pious works excite our pride; health excites our passions, sickness nourishes lukewarmness or murmurings.

Whatever it is that most often tempts us and holds us the fastest, that betrays us most frequently into the hands of Satan, that brings us into a daily or an hourly fall, we must find it out and conquer it. It is necessary that we do this. We must not let one sin, be it ever so small in our eyes, stand between us and God, in whose Eye no sin is small; with whom all sins are hateful. We must not let one sin, however besetting, however much we may be enslaved to it, stand between the soul and its Saviour. For we are solemnly warned by the Apostle that "whosoever shall keep the whole law, and yet offend in one point, he is guilty of all" (St. James, 2-10). This is almost a staggering—almost a fearful bit of information. No matter how good we are in other particulars; no matter how obediently we keep all other commandments; no matter how faithful we may be in all other things, if we sin in one particular, violate one obligation, break one commandment, "offend in one point," even if it be the least, "we are guilty of all." So far as God is concerned we might as well offend in all as only in one; one sin will bring His wrath upon us as much as if we were guilty of the whole catalogue of sins. There is no degree in His wrath, as there is no gradation in punishment. It is with God either love or wrath, either forgiveness or punishment; and it matters not if the sin be one or manifold, gross or small. "If we offend in one point, we are guilty of all."

We therefore see how necessary it is that we—you and I—shall "lay aside every weight," everything of a sinful nature that keeps back the soul in its race for the "crown of life;" especially that we lay aside and put far from us "the sin that doth so easily beset us."

So long as we live in this world, we cannot be without temptation. "The life of man is a life of temptation." So long as we live, therefore, we shall always need to defend ourselves on every side, lest the devil find an advantage to deceive us; for he never sleepeth, and therefore we should be ever watching. For no man is so perfect and holy but he has sometimes temptations, and we cannot be altogether without them. Therefore all the more wakeful and watchful we must be; all the more prayerful—watching in prayer—remembering two things:

First, that "it is no sin to be tempted; nor is our being tempted any proof of our being sinful." It is proof only of our being human; of our being pursued, attacked, assaulted with a devouring greed by Satan. More than this it may not, and need not, prove. The temptation, whatever it may be, however cunning and however fierce, may glance off like the poisoned arrow from the well-poised shield; and will glance off if we watch in prayer, leaving us purified by the encounter, and stronger than all our enemies. But remember:

Secondly, when we consent to a temptation it becomes a sin. When we yield, we take it into the heart; it becomes a part of our nature. So long as we do not consent, do not yield, no matter what the temptation may be, however besetting, it remains outside of us and harmless. But when we give assent, it enters the soul, however swept and garnished the soul may have been; and darkens, defiles, pollutes it, perhaps for all time to come and for all eternity.

How needful, then, that you and I should be ever watchful against temptation, especially against "the sin that doth so easily beset us;" that so often brings us to defeat and a fall! How necessary that we lay it aside; that we think of it in the morning to fortify ourselves against it, and think of it at night to confess it if we have fallen! For unless we put it, and all sins from us, we shall not come to eternal light, since only "the pure in heart shall see God."

EIGHTH DAY OF LENT.

Sins Which Crucify Christ.

They crucify to themselves the Son of God afresh, and put Him to an open shame.—Hebrews vi. 6.

THIS is a sad state, indeed, of which the Apostle tells us. It brings to our mind, on the one hand, the crucifixion of our Lord on Calvary; it brings to mind all those sad circumstances in that last sorrowful week of His Life; it calls to our remembrance the stupendous sacrifice on the Cross—the infinite love that willed it, and the sins that made it necessary. As we look upon that Cross, and think of that suffering, that love, and those sins, many of the pleadings of our Lord come to mind—and many of His woes. "How often would I have gathered thy children together, even as a hen gathers her chickens under her wings, and ye would not."

What a longing this was for the love of those for whom the Love of His Heart was shed in Sacrifice! But they would not love; no, not even for the sake of that which He had for them: "Ye will not come to Me that ye may have life." He was that life; but they neither came to Him, nor loved Him. They only mocked, and scourged, and crucified Him. The Life which He had to give them for their eternal peace, they took in the bitterness of hatred and in cold blood. Every sin, from Christ to Adam, was confederated in the hammering of those cruel nails, and the thrusting of that piercing spear. And all these sins He saw, and felt, when He pronounced those bitter woes: "Woe unto thee, Chorazin, woe unto thee, Bethsaida;" "woe unto the world because of offences;" "woe to that man by whom the offence is committed;" "woe unto you, Scribes and Pharisees, hypocrites;" "woe unto that man by whom the Son of Man is betrayed." All those sins which He saw and felt, from Adam down, forced from His pale lips those agonizing cries of "woe." For what was to be punishment to them, was pain and grief to Him.

But He did not alone look back over the world for the sins that made Him suffer such torture of Body and Soul. Not alone the sins from Adam down to these last tormentors at the foot of His Cross, were present to His Soul, as He suffered this last cruel agony of His Life. No! Ours, too, He saw and felt, as He was uplifted on the Cross. He looked into the future, and saw all the myriad sins that would yet be committed. He looked into our own hearts, and saw—as He sees now—all the evil and all the sin that we try to hide. He looked to the very end of the world, and saw all the wickedness that should be in it to the last. All this was present to His Soul. In His Divine Ommiscience, He was vividly conscious of the sins of the whole world, from the Creation to the end. And the sense of this, more than the insults of the mob or the sufferings of His Body, made His "Soul exceeding sorrowful even unto death." Our sins, and the sins of to-day, no less than the sins committed in the days of Noah; the sins of this community no less than the sins of

Chorazin and Bethsaida, or of Sodom and Gomorrah, were leading the Lamb of God to His slaughter on Calvary. "He was wounded for our transgressions; He was bruised for our iniquities."

But have we ever thought of this? Have we ever thought that our hands helped to plait that crown of thorns, and to drive those nails? Have we ever thought that we crucified our dear Lord and Saviour? Not only may we look back and see the crucifixion for which our sins are responsible; many—very many, to-day, perhaps some of us among the number, "crucify to themselves the Son of God afresh, and put Him to an open shame." Many—very many, to-day, inflict some new pang upon Him; pierce His Heart with a fresh pang of sorrow; revive and repeat the torture of the Cross. And among those who thus keep on erecting crosses for our Lord's crucifixion, who thus continue the shame of His sufferings and the bitterness of His anguish, may be some of us.

Does it seem to you that, because He has ascended on high, He can feel no grief? That, because He has been taken up into glory, He can experience no pain and sorrow? False notion of our Saviour's love and sympathy! "We have not an High Priest which cannot be touched with the feeling of our infirmities;" and He who could weep, in the keenness of His sympathy, when on earth, for the sorrow and distress of His people, can now be moved by the sight of grief and suffering. If He can, from His throne, behold our sorrows and sufferings; if in His exaltation, He can feel our grief; if, in His home of glory, He can "be touched with the feeling of our infirmities;" He can also be pained by the sight of human sin, and, through His power of suffering, be "crucified afresh" by those deeds of darkness which men now commit—those "deeds that are evil" which we commit. Not only, in His Divine Omniscience, does He look down and behold the sins of His people, and in His infinite sympathy suffer pain because of our sins; but our sins rise up to Him in Heaven, and there cry out against us. Oh! terrible thought, that God not only sees the evil in our hearts, but that our sins cry unto God from the ground; not only put Him to an open shame here, but in the very home of glory send a piercing shaft through His Sacred Heart.

But, according to the Apostle, it is not every sin that crucifies the Son of God afresh. He mentions only one—the sin of apostasy; and yet it is possible that all sins may at last be gathered up in this one. "It is impossible," says he, "for those who were once enlightened, and have tasted of the heavenly gift, and were made partakers of the Holy Ghost, and have tasted the good word of God, and the powers of the world to come, if they shall fall away, to renew them again unto repentance; seeing they crucify unto themselves the Son of God afresh, and put Him to an open shame."

Apostasy means a standing off, an abandonment of what one has voluntarily professed, a total desertion or departure from one's faith. It cannot be that there are any such here—any who have abandoned their Christian profession and deserted their Lord. Such are not usually found in Church during Lent. But there are degrees of departure. And may it not be that some of us, while not going the full length of an apostate, have yet taken some steps in that direction; that some of us have in some measure "fallen away" from that white heat of faith and profession, which brought us to our Confirmation. You shudder at the thought of such little apostasies, and think it impossible for you to sin thus. St. Peter thought so, and before the cock crew he had denied his Lord thrice. Others, who had been far advanced in the narrow way; who had grown much in grace; who had tasted often the heavenly gift, and found it sweet; who had known much comfort and peace in the Holy Ghost; nevertheless fell, and added nails and thorns to their Lord's passion, and pierced again and again His pure and loving Soul. And if they could, why may not we? "Let him that thinketh he standeth take heed lest he fall."

Think of the much backsliding that is done—that we have done; now tasting that the Lord is gracious, and then falling under a strong temptation; now being lifted in the power of the Spirit to the blessedness of life, and then coquetting with Satan and playing on the edge of the precipice overhanging hell. Heirs of unending life,—candidates for eternity, and hastening towards its awful realities,—tabernacled by Christ and His Holy Spirit; we yet, now and again, turn aside, and amuse ourselves with lying vanities and sport with our own deceivings, upon Eternity's dreadful brink. We hear Christ assailed, His Church ridiculed, His Faith antagonized, His religion despised, His people mocked,—and we are silent as the grave. We hear our Lord falsely accused, denied, blasphemed, crucified by His enemies around us; and in the cowardice of our hearts, by our silence, we desert Him, too, and "crucify Him afresh." The opportunity is given us to confess Him before men, but we backslide and hold our peace. He looks to us for aid in the war against Satan, but we add intensity to the bitterness of His sorrow by wounding Him in the house of His own familiar friend. Not this alone; when His table is spread with the Divine Feast, many of us—communicants of the Church—turn our backs on the Feast of the Altar, and, instead of coming to Him, weary and heavy laden with our sins, go out from Him, who offers Himself for our Peace. Oh! to be so near to Him, and yet to pass Him by; to know Him in all His beauty, and yet to "crucify Him afresh;" to bear His image, and yet to "put Him to an open shame;" to be exalted to heaven,—to be thrust down to hell! What a height,—what a depth! And then when we stand before Him at the Great Day, and ask Him the meaning of those wounds in His Body, to hear Him say: "Those with which I was wounded in the house of My friends"—those which *thou* hast inflicted upon Me!

NINTH DAY OF LENT.

Death.

The wages of sin is Death.—Rom. vi. 23.

WE have so far in our Lent meditations thought upon sin, sins of habit and sins of character; what they are in themselves, and what they are to God and to us; how they develop, how hateful and sinful they are, and how they crucify Christ. Let us to-day think upon that which sin has brought into the world, "the wages of sin," that is, Death. "As by one man sin entered into the world, and death by sin, so death passed upon all men, for that all have sinned."

"Sin," says one, "is the blindness of our minds, the perverseness and crookedness of our wills, and the monstrous irregularity and disorder of our affections and appetites."[*]

"Sin," says another, "as a raging and commandding king, has the sinner's heart for his throne; the members of the body for its service; the world, the flesh and the devil for its grand council; lusts and temptations for its weapons and armory; and its fortifications are ignorance, sensuality and fleshly reasonings."[†]

Death—physical, spiritual, eternal, all the collected

---

[*]Tillotson.
[†]Burkitt.

evil results of sin—comes as the punishment of sin; and puts an end to the work, but not an end to the worker. Sin and death are cause and effect. If Adam had not sinned, he might have been "clothed upon" by a kiss of the Almighty, with higher forms of being; but the prophet's words—"the soul that sinneth it shall die"—were uttered beside the forbidden tree in the Garden; and Adam sinned and died. And so have all since died that have come into the world.

Days pass into weeks, weeks into months, months into years. The one ends as does the other; and as they end so does life. Life is but a span long and age is as nothing in respect of eternity. How fast does time fly! How quickly do the days, and the weeks, and the months, and the years glide away! How soon will this poor, short life come to an end! "We bring our years to an end as it were a tale that is told;" they dissipate into a dream that is past, and we hasten on to that moment which is for each the end of time, the beginning of eternity.

The question has often been asked: Is life worth living? It is looked at as a speculation, and the question with most persons is: What return shall I get for the outlay? Does it pay? And the answer will depend on the life itself. If life be selfish, seeking pleasure, ardent for the world, its fame and fortune, inflamed by our worldly attachments and desires, reanimated by our passions, steeped in sin and covered with shame, it will surely not pay. The sooner it comes to its end the better; but what an end that is! Yet, if lived for God and in God's light, keeping His commandments and doing His will, the end will be blessed.

But do we so live that this may be our end? "It is appointed unto all men once to die." Let us look our end in the face and ask that question. Do we live as they whose "soul doth wait for the Lord?"

Many of us may have seen death. All have no doubt stood beside a grave. We have seen birth, youth, manhood, titles, fame, wither in a moment, and forever buried in the grave. We have been impressed with the certainty of death and the reality of a future. Yet we go from a melancholy grave into the busy world as if we were to live and labor through eternal ages. We return from a death scene into the world more occupied with, and more eager for, those vain things of this life, the insignificance and meanness of which we had but so lately seen with our own eyes. What blindness! What folly! We lay projects, assume cares, form attachments, stretch every nerve in the pursuit of fortune and rank; we heap up riches and gratify our ambitions; yet the money for which we toiled and sinned, in thinking of which we forgot God, and the sinful pleasures for which we sacrificed our souls, all must be left at death's door. Nothing but our true nature, our real character, ourselves as we are, can pass beyond. We fear, and we reproach ourselves, lest we never do enough for ourselves and our worldly affairs; but we check ourselves in the dread of doing too much for an eternal fortune. Nothing is too much for the world; but in the fear of doing too much for God we do nothing at all—in the fear of doing too much for our salvation we neglect it entirely. Because it is not certain that we shall die to-day, we live as if we were to live forever. Such a life; blind, foolish, mad, intoxicated with the world's pleasures, and deceived by its illusions, does certainly not pay, and is not worth living.

There is nothing so certain, and so uncertain, as death. The first step which man takes in life, is likewise the first towards the grave. The first breath he takes is laden with the poison of sin. Death is uncertain, and therefore it is imprudent to forget its coming and to let it surprise us. Death is certain, and therefore it is foolish to dread the thought of it and to keep it out of sight. It is uncertain, because we know not the hour, nor the day, nor even the year of its coming, though it may come to-morrow. Death is certain; it must happen; it is written on our bodies; we carry in our breasts its slow poison, which is corrupting and undermining our health, and will one day extinguish the feeble and flickering flame of our life.

Death "cometh as a thief in the night"—but it cometh. Both its certainty and its uncertainty should cause us to give our thought and our prayer to it. But that day is seldom in our minds. We live, and that is sufficient. We live as if we should live forever. Upon what do we calculate long life? In what do we trust, that we so utterly neglect the thought of our last hour? In youth? It is indeed full of hope, and promise, and possibilities. But the son of the widow of Nain was young; others around us seemingly certain of long life, have been smitten in the flower of youth so that they perished. Or, in the strength of your constitution? Yet a single day's sickness is enough to lay on a bed of pain and suffering the strongest among us. The best health is but a spark which a breath may extinguish. What madness, then, to build our hopes of long life on youth or health, and neglect the only certain thing that is appointed unto us.

Think, then, upon death; and think how different the death of the sinner and the death of the righteous.

The one may have filled the world with his name; history with his deeds; monuments may not hold all the acts of his life; fortune may have poured upon him a continued shower of successes; honored and sung of all men, and glorious in the eyes of all. But in the sight of God he may be the vilest of mortals. He has lived only for self and vanity; immortal in the world's annals, but he has nothing deserving written in the Book of Eternity, and nothing but shame and disgrace following him into the presence of God. He trusted, perhaps, that before death should look him in the face he should overcome the sin of his soul; but he hugged its pollutions closer to his bosom. He thought, perhaps, of the fate of the sinner who dies in his sins; but he tranquilly prepares himself for the same fate. He wishes to die the death of a saint, and to live the life of a sinner. His life is full of good desires and intentions, but empty of good works. When his last end comes, having lived a stranger to God, he can now offer Him nothing but his sins. His earthly pleasures, hopes, transactions, vanish like a dream; but he remains to give account of them. Everything around his bedside, every turn of his thoughts brings back to his mind some sin long forgotten. The heavens and the earth rise up against him, and unfold to him the sinful story of his life. He despairs of God's clemency; feels himself unworthy of His mercies; is told by a secret voice in his own heart, of the hopeless state of the impious; and his soul, pronounced Christian at his Baptism, sealed with the sign of salvation which he effaced, purified by grace which he trampled under foot, admitted to a profession which he has always profaned;—that soul, with groans of agony and cries of despair, with eyes growing dark and gloomy, with convulsions and quiverings, passes out of its crumbling clay and falls into the hands of its God, who, with tears and sighing, thrusts it into the blackness of darkness forever.

Far different is the death of the man of God. He lives in the fear of God, and in the love of God; and he dies as he lives. Life is full of trials, temptations, dangers; full of disquiet and distress, of tears and combats and defeats; death is deliverance and perpetual peace. It is the day of the Lord's coming, and he meets death with a song of praise and thanksgiving; for he shall be clothed upon with immortality and enter the society of those holy ones who are seated around the Throne in the ineffable brightness of God's countenance. He leaves a perishing world, which he has never loved, and sees the bosom of Abraham opening to receive him. He is borne by blessed spirits into that habitation; and you, who remain and see him fall asleep, are forced to exclaim: "Blessed are the dead who die in the Lord."

Imagine your own death. It cannot be difficult to imagine. You are sick, and grow weaker. Medicines will not help you. You grow still weaker, and there is danger. Then there is great danger. Then there is no hope. Then all is over. How would you meet it? Dare you face it? If you could not with confidence face it now, how do you know you can when it does come? A life's work cannot be done on a death-bed.

Life, not death itself, is the preparation for death; and as a man lives so shall he die.

Think of death, of your life as a preparation for it. Happy if you die in the Lord; eternally wretched if you depart in sin.

TENTH DAY OF LENT.

THE JUDGMENT.

The great day of His wrath is come; and who shall be able to stand?—Romans vi. 17.

OUR last meditation was upon death. We have seen what a terrible day, a day of wrath, it will be to the impenitent and wicked, and what a glad and happy day to the holy; a day of sadness and gloom to the one, and to the other a birthday to a better life in a better world. There is one more scene, equally terrible to the one and equally blessed to the other, and equally certain to all.

"Immediately after the tribulation of those days shall the sun be darkened, and the moon shall not give her light, and the stars shall fall from heaven, and the powers of the heavens shall be shaken; and then shall appear the sign of the Son of Man in the heavens, and they shall see the Son of Man coming in the clouds of heaven with power and great glory."

"When the Son of Man shall come in his glory, and all the holy angels with Him, then shall He sit upon the throne of His glory. And before Him shall be gathered all nations; and He shall separate them one from another, as a shepherd divideth the sheep from the goats. And He shall set the sheep on His right hand, but the goats on His left. Then shall the King say unto them on His right hand: Come, ye blessed of my Father, inherit the Kingdom prepared for you from the foundation of the world. Then shall He also say unto them on the left hand: Depart from me, ye cursed, into everlasting fire, prepared for the devil and his angels. And these shall go away into everlasting punishment, but the righteous into life eternal."

On earth all things come alike to sinners and saints. God's mercies are poured out with an open hand, and they fall all around without regard to those who receive them. He is the Father of all, and careth for all. Even so are all men free to make the most of themselves and their opportunities. The world of business is as a problem of evolution; and the fittest man, he with greater powers of endurance, survives in the struggle for place or fortune. The righteous and the wicked, the good and the bad, the clean and the unclean, they that sacrifice and they that sacrifice not, have all an equal chance before God and man. Not so in the Great Day. Men will be neither equal before God, nor will they have a like chance to obtain His favor and blessing on that day of great revelations.

But picture the scene, a scene that is fast coming, and coming to all of us. It will be but a faint picture at the best; for with all our powers of imagination we cannot conceive of it. Imagine a mighty space, far as the eye can see, nay, far as the mind can reach, spread out before you; filled with a mighty throng of human beings, a vast and numberless army of souls, living and dead, small and great, infant and adult, young and old, countless millions of human forms; ranks and legions and wondrous multitudes;

peoples, tribes and nations; worlds upon worlds of human souls stretching away in one vast and awful and amazing array. And somewhere in this mighty host will be you and I.

But all eyes are fixed upon one central scene, glorious yet terrible to behold. A "great white throne resting upon the clouds of heaven," surrounded by the holy angels; and seated upon it One whose "visage was so marred more than any man, and His form more than the sons of men;" yet whose very look, by its seriousness and the awful solemnity of His countenance, strikes doubt or terror into every heart. All eyes are fixed upon Him, with varied look yet in speechless awe; some, who have known and confessed Him that sitteth on the Throne, look with pleasure and delight upon Him whom they have long wished to see; others, and by far the greater number, who have denied Him before men, seeing His holiness and their own sinfulness, would now turn away from His gaze and hide from His anger if they could, knowing that He now will deny them before the Father. Somewhere in this mighty host will be you and I.

But this central Figure in this mighty assembly is not the most terrible thing on this most terrible Day. More dreadful to think about is the fact that, before this Holy Being on His Throne, will be spread all the history of our life. Everything will be unfolded before Him, from our first breath to our last sigh. All the iniquities of our whole life will confront us. All the misdeeds and shortcomings, all the crimes secret and open, all the vanity and obstinacy and weaknesses and meannesses, will be collected before our eyes and before His searching gaze. Not an act, not a wish or desire, not a word or thought will be omitted. And, if the very hair of our head be numbered, think of our deeds. "Our iniquities are set before Him, the most secret sins in the light of His countenance." "There is nothing covered, that shall not be revealed; and hid, that shall not be known." And "if Thou, Lord, wilt be extreme to mark what is done amiss, O Lord, who may abide it?"

But this is not all that we see on this dreadful Day, in this mighty army of human beings. We see this vast multitude part; there is a quick and busy movement on all sides; we see it form again in two great companies, in two mighty armies, one on the right hand and one on the left of the Son of Man seated upon His Throne. The one give every sign of surprise, despair, terror, and confusion; the other have the marks of serenity, confidence, and bliss on their countenance. The one look toward the Throne with confident expectation of life eternal and bliss everlasting; the other, with quivering frame, and eyes fixed downward as if piercing the abyss which is yawning toward them, gasp with horror and would escape if they could. The "King of Glory," looking from His Throne with eyes full of love and sweetness, will say to those on the one side the words of consolation and peace: "Come, ye blessed of My Father, inherit the Kingdom prepared for you from the foundation of the world." But to those on His left, with changed countenance, with eyes full of vengeance and fury, and voice which shall burst open the bowels of the abyss to swallow them up, He shall say,—not, "come, ye blessed," nor, as from the

Cross, "Father, forgive them," but, "Depart from Me, ye cursed, into everlasting fire, prepared for the devil and his angels." Somewhere in this scene, on the one side or the other, hearing these words that shall assign us to a lot which shall change no more, which shall be for ever and ever and ever, will be you and I.

You say, perhaps, you have not been given power to overcome; that you were brought into this world weak in body, with a temperament prone to the evil which God abhors, with a heart susceptible to all the temptations which beset the soul. You say, perhaps, that God has not given you sufficient grace to battle against the odds in which He has placed you. But in that bright and clear light which shall then be cast into the soul, revealing everything not only to the Eye of God, nor only to us, but which will enable the host of human beings around to see what we are, we will then see that our whole life has been one of abuses of God's grace, one of resistance to the opportunities and privileges which He has held out to us, one of continued quenching of His Holy Spirit, one of trifling with divine inspirations and of neglect of sacramental nourishment. We will then see how great things God hath done for our salvation, and how little we ourselves have done to aid God's grace in our behalf.

Were this scene to break upon us now; were this Day to open now; were we now caught up and set before the Throne and searched through and through by that piercing glance of the All-seeing Eye, on which side would we find ourselves? How would we appear before that awful tribunal? With what feelings would we behold the Face of the Son of God? What could we expect from Him? The Book of the Law still lays its threatenings and its pleadings and its promises before us: "Children of Israel, behold I set before you this day a blessing and a curse; a blessing, if ye obey the commandment of the Lord your God which I command you this day; and a curse, if ye obey not the commandments of the Lord your God, but turn aside, out of the way which I command you this day, to go after other gods which ye have not known." The right hand and the left are before us, the promises and the threatenings, the blessings and the curses, the path that leads to life and the path which leads to everlasting perdition. In which path are you now? On which side will you be then? "Choose you this day whom ye will serve; whether the God of your Fathers, or the gods of the Amorites in whose land ye dwell." Whichever be your choice, in your morning and your night watches, forget not this last and terrible scene, and the part which you will play in it.

ELEVENTH DAY OF LENT.

Eternity.

Thus saith the high and lofty One who inhabiteth eternity.—Isaiah lvii. 15.

LET us to-day meditate upon Eternity. What a tremendous theme it is; full of mysteries concerning God, and angels, and ourselves, and the states called heaven and hell! What an immensity the word brings to mind! It almost makes the mind stagger to think about it. Vast in its length and breadth—we have nothing in this universe that can give us the faintest idea of it. It is impossible for us to define the word so as to tell really what it is. We say it is the dwelling-place of the Almighty; yet who can form an adequate conception of it? We say it is everlasting—endless; yet who can conceive of anything endless? We say it is a very, very long time—millions upon millions of years; yet it is not time, and it is not years. We say the whole duration of time is, to Eternity, as one grain of sand is to the whole globe, or as one drop of water is to the mighty ocean; but, try to conceive of it, and you are lost in thought—in wonder and amazement. Only He who inhabiteth Eternity can know what it is. We can only think of the word in awe; and, as for the thing itself, it is past human thought. We look back over the world's history, and think six thousand years to

Adam a very long time. We excavate ancient cities, and dig up remains of inscriptions which we think very ancient; which tell us about people we never heard of, and about events which we never knew of. Yet it takes nearly one hundred and sixty-seven times six thousand to make a million; and eternity is a million million—millions upon millions of years. And the end of this million times million—millions upon millions of years—may be but the beginning of Eternity. What a boundless, awful, stupendous conception the word Eternity brings to mind!

Space is one of the things that make our universe. But think of space, who can? The mind travels to the sun, which is ninety-one millions of miles from us; and then on to the nearest fixed star, which is two hundred thousand times farther from us than the sun. And there are millions of stars beyond this, millions of times still further from us. What a marvellous immensity we are entering into! Yet there is an end to space, as there will be to Time. But who can conceive of the end of space, as he travels on from star to star, and sees a countless number of stars farther beyond? So still more marvellous in extent and duration is Eternity. If we can conceive of no end to space, which is finite, how can we conceive of Eternity, which is infinite! On the outside of Earth man stands, with the boundless heaven above him, space around him and above him—nothing but space. We wonder in silence and amazement. So still more do we wonder and tremble at the thought of Eternity.

Think of Eternity as God's Dwelling-place. Think of all its secrets and wonders. "Eye hath not seen, nor ear heard, neither have entered into the heart of man, the things which God hath prepared for them that love Him;" and all these are hid in that boundless, that endless, place called Eternity, and will one day be revealed unto us in all their splendor and glory. That wondrous world, with its "many mansions," its "inheritance, incorruptible and undefiled, and that fadeth not away," its "crown of righteousness which the Lord will give," will one day lay its secrets before us, and its best treasures will be our own. The manifold forms in which the All-Beautiful has concealed His Essence; the Living Garment in which the Invisible has clothed His mysterious loveliness, are revealed above the sky and in the eternity beyond; and we shall behold with rapturous gaze, and be forever satisfied in the contemplation.

Think, also, of those blessed beings who, with God, inhabit eternity. Thrones, dominions, principalities, and powers; angels and archangels; patriarchs and prophets; apostles, martyrs, confessors, and saints of all ages; "a great multitude which no man can number, of all nations, and kindreds, and people and tongues," all dwell with God in light, and stand "before the throne, and before the Lamb, clothed with white robes, and palms in their hands, and cry with a loud voice, saying, Salvation unto our God which sitteth upon the throne, and unto the Lamb." "In the beauty of holiness," in the brightness of Glory, in the fulness of happiness, in the light of God's countenance, in the Divine smile, "they cry one to the other, Holy, holy, holy is the Lord of hosts: the whole earth is full of His glory;" and "they rest not day nor night, saying, Holy, holy,

holy Lord God Almighty, which was, and is, and is to come."

Think, too, what a glorious heritage they have, who dwell with God in Eternity, and worship Him. "They have come out of great tribulation, and have washed their robes and made them white in the blood of the Lamb. They shall hunger no more, neither thirst any more; neither shall the sun light on them, nor any heat. For the Lamb which is in the midst of the throne shall feed them, and shall lead them unto living fountains of water: and God shall wipe away all tears from their eyes;" "and there shall be no more death, neither sorrow, nor crying, neither shall there be any more pain; for the former things are passed away."

This is but a faint and poor picture of God's Dwelling-place, in which saints and angels find peace and happiness, and worship the Lamb that sitteth upon the throne. Far as the east is from the west, wide as virtue differs from vice, much as the noonday sun surpasses in light and splendor the feeble flame of a candle, vast as the universe is in comparison with this earth, so the glories of Eternity far exceed all that we can imagine or desire.

For this Eternity you and I were created; for it we are destined; towards it we are going—fast, fast going—each day's end bringing us one day nearer that moment when we, as I hope, shall awake up in the brightness of eternal glory. Its very shadow is even now upon us. We shall live forever. Immortal as God Himself who made us, we, too, shall inhabit Eternity. "Though worms destroy this body, yet in the flesh shall we see God," and dwell with Him, and worship Him, and minister to Him, in His everlasting Home of peace and glory. Worlds pass away; but the soul lives on, and on, forever. Myriads of ages pass away; but the soul is no nearer the end of its existence than it was at the beginning. Endless existence! Eternity! What awful thoughts! What a marvellous destiny! You and I shall live on, and on, forever and ever, with all the saints, in the Dwelling-place of the Most High God, or else—shall we say it?—in the bottomless pit of perdition.

Do we ever think of Eternity as not only God's Home, but as our own? Are our hearts set upon it? Do we love to reflect about it, and do we earnestly hope and long for it? Has it a charm for our hearts? Are our affections set on the things therein, and not on things on the earth? Do we say, with David: "Like as the hart desireth the water-brooks, so longeth my soul after Thee, O God?" Is our soul, like David's, "athirst for God, yea, for the living God?" Do we say, with St. Paul, that we are "willing rather to be absent from the body and to be present with the Lord?" Do we say, with David, "out of the deep" "I look for the Lord: my soul doth wait for Him; in His word is my trust. My soul fleeth unto the Lord before the morning watch, I say before the morning watch." Oh, the secrets, and the mysteries, and the glorious things that are contained in Eternity, that are prepared by the High and Lofty One for those who love Him!

Many do not think of Eternity; but they live regardless of it. They live solely for Time. Their thoughts are so wrapped up in this world, that they think not of the next. They are wholly given up to the cares and interests of temporal things, and are forgetful of the things that are eternal. What are all the beauties of nature, what is all the glory of this world, compared to that heavenly world where the Godhead dwells? Oh, to have gained all the pleasures and comforts afforded in Space and Time, but to have with it lost Eternity!—to have gained the whole world, but to have lost his own soul!

I repeat, therefore, has Eternity any charm for us? Do we love to think about it, and long for the time when its light shall dawn upon us? Time shall be no more; earth and sea and sky shall be blotted out; but we shall live forever. Amazing folly and madness *not* to think of that forever of glory, or forever of torment whither we are all going; and more than madness not to set our affections on things above.

Think yet again. In these many mansions of the Father's House, will there be one prepared for you and for me? Will you, will I, be in the Kingdom? Will our eyes behold "the King in His beauty?" There can be no doubt as to who will be there. Patriarchs and prophets, and all the holy men of old; apostles, martyrs, confessors, and saints of all ages; hosts of poor and nameless believers in the Lord, who have in patience borne the sorrows of life; myriads of holy ones who have lived in steadfast faith, and died in a sure hope of a blessed immortality; "the holy Church throughout all the world," redeemed out of all mankind, and triumphant forevermore;—these all shall be there, in garments of spotless white, and singing the songs of salvation around the throne; but will you be there, and will I? Let the question sink deep into our hearts, because it deals with awful realities: When the Lord gathers the elect into His Kingdom, will you be there, and will I?

TWELFTH DAY OF LENT.

Self-Examination.

Examine yourselves, whether ye be in the faith; prove your own selves.—II Corinthians xiii. 5.

WHAT man is there who has not sore need of such examination and proving? Who among us has not within his breast something that must cause apprehension or fear? The best of us is not beyond God's indignation, and "the righteous scarcely are saved." There is often something which the cloak of charity cannot cover, nor the perfume of good words and good deeds hide. Look to-day into your heart and see if there be any wickedness in it; prove your soul and see if there be any good in it. For we may imagine ourselves to be in the faith when we are not; and we who deceive ourselves in this matter, so essential to our everlasting salvation, are criminally guilty for it, God having made it the privilege and the duty of every man, by faithful examination, to ascertain with confidence whether he is in the faith or not. Look to-day over your past life; scan every year, every month, every day if possible, and see and prove your own selves in the clear light of honest and earnest search down in the very bottom of your heart; in the most remote recesses of your soul, for those faults of your life, those shortcomings, those sins which have held you and marked you before God and man. See and search and prove to-day, as you must see and prove some day, where, in all God's Kingdom, you love to stand.

Look! Oh, those sins we have committed, you and I; and that corrupt nature from which they have all sprung! Oh, that deep-seated, unconquerable desire of our hearts to have our own will, and to live our own way! See the many, many evils we have committed in God's sight, and the many, many things, great and small, which we have left undone. See the many careless or evil habits into which we have fallen. See those sins of character which are part of ourselves—our pride, anger, covetousness, selfishness, hypocrisy, and such like, which are seated on the throne of our hearts—yours and mine—and, great God! those hearts are Temples of the Holy Spirit! With what fear must we look and prove ourselves, in the face of such startling disclosures as the slightest examination of our hearts and our lives must make! How constantly do we fail to carry out what it is manifestly intended we should as sons of God and children of light! How often do we resolve to take Christ to be our Master, and pledge Him our hearty obedience; that He alone shall rule our hearts; that He alone shall be King over us; that His Law shall be our meditation and our delight; that He shall be the pattern of our lives; that the beauty of His saintliness shall be our model! But when He takes our promise and our pledge, and comes to abide in us, to dwell in our hearts as His home and make it in all things pleasing to Himself, how constantly and, alas! how quickly do we forget our promise, and seek another's dominion! How constantly and how quickly do we fail Him when He most needs us, and turn a deaf ear to even the earliest of His commands! How often in the morning do we dedicate ourselves to God, and when with the burden and heat of the day the trial comes, instantly forget it! How often have we prayed for grace to overcome habits or to withstand temptations, and have quickly fallen back into them again! How sorely disappointed He must be, how bitterly grieved at our unfaithfulness and our unworthiness, our fitful fluctuations and our falseness! "Deceitful above all things and desperately wicked" will we find our hearts if we will but stop and look, and "examine and prove our own selves;" if we will but "consider the days of old and the years that are past." And so will God find them and look upon them with the sorrow of His soul.

Looking upon us now, does He find faith in us? Does His searching Eye find anywhere in our hearts anything to love and bless? Where and what is it? Where and what are its tokens? Do faith and love inspire all our actions, and shine forth out of all our words? Do we feed upon God's Truth; and feed our souls with heavenly Manna as eagerly as we feed our bodies with the food that perishes?

So might we continue to ask ourselves, so might we continue examining and proving ourselves by God's Word and God's Commandments. But the answer must in all cases come back with startling force: Nay, we have come short, far short of God's lowest expectations. We have broken all our promises, and violated all our obligations. Thus do we stand before ourselves and before God self-confessed and self-condemned.

Oh, if we should go on day by day, and year by year, as, by self-examination, we have proven ourselves to be! Or, if we should go on thus, without ever examining and proving our own selves; our faults and our sins unconfessed, unrepented, unforgiven; great God, what a debt we should owe Thee! And if we should never know them until we should hear of them from His own Mouth at the Last and Great Day, Most Merciful God, what shadow of hope could there be for us! If, therefore, we should be afraid to die with our sins unknown, unconfessed, unrepented and unforgiven, why should we not be afraid to live in that frightful state of soul? If, on our death-bed, we should hurry into confession and repentance; if, then, in the night of death, we should "prove our own selves," and lay our sins before a merciful God with a prayer for forgiveness, why not do so each night, with each day's sins, and pray for pardon and grace to amend?

If we would not so die, let us not so live. "Examine yourselves, whether ye be in the faith; prove your own selves," whether ye be in the Covenant; whether ye love God with all your heart and soul, and are in perfect charity with all mankind. What better time to do it than this? What better time to search out and confess our sins against our neighbor, what better time to lay bare our sins against God? We balance all our accounts with our fellow-man; why not do so with God? We look earnestly into all our worldly affairs, and watch the state of our money matters; why not examine into all our past words and deeds, even our thoughts and secret faults, and prove the state of our souls? What better time to do so than this?

Let us examine ourselves, therefore, you and I, as God will one day examine us—you and me. What if we should come before Him without a single thought of our sins! What if He should call us before His bar with every stain on our souls, the great and the small, unwashed!—if He should see us, who are creatures of but an hour, yet defiled by ten thousand times ten thousand sins and offences! Oh, the pain to His Heart, and the remorse to our souls, if we should find ourselves, because of offences that may be unforgiven and sins that may not be covered, outside the power of human prayers, or, if possible, of Divine mercy! Let us shake off the sloth and idleness which hold us captive, and, looking into our hearts, let us reckon up the debt we owe God; and then, overwhelmed with the sense of our sinfulness and our utter unworthiness, let us come to God for pardon—to the Fountain for uncleanness for that cleansing and purifying which all must have who long to "see the King in His beauty," and to feel the welcoming pressure of His loving, guiding Hand, and to live in the Light of His countenance forever and ever.

THIRTEENTH DAY OF LENT.

Repentance.

Repent ye, for the Kingdom of Heaven is at hand.—St. Matthew iii. 2.

THE first word of both the Baptist in the wilderness and of Christ when He entered upon His mission, was a cry to repentance; a call to a change of mind and of heart—a change of life and of purpose in life. For, said they both, "the Kingdom of Heaven is at hand;" and "except ye repent, ye shall all perish;" except we "repent, and believe the Gospel" we cannot be delivered from our sins and be saved.

If we have "examined ourselves whether we be in the faith, and proven our own selves;" if we have searched our own hearts, and looked earnestly into the lowest depths and the remotest and darkest chambers of the soul; and dragged into the light of conscience, and before God's Eye, all its sins and evils, all its secret faults and open transgressions, all its hidden and long-forgotten wickednesses as well as its most recent disobediences, we must know well the necessity for repentance; and we must be moved to repentance by even the slightest "proving" of our inward state; we must be covered with the shame and confusion of our own wickedness and unworthiness, and seek, close by the sin-laden Cross, the comforting compassion and pardon that follow repentance as surely as day follows the darkness of night, or as calm follows the severest storm, or as peace follows the decisive battle.

Repentance has two parts; it is a two-fold act of the mind and heart. It is a turning from sin in godly sorrow, and a turning to God with a full purpose of amendment. We must therefore need to know our state and the way of deliverance from it; we must know our need and the source of succour. We must know and confess that "we have sinned against the Lord our God, we and our fathers, from our youth even unto this day, and have not obeyed the voice of the Lord our God; and then we must "turn unto the Lord our God with weeping, fasting and mourning" —with contrition, confession, and a hearty resolution to do God's will.

One of the first things for us, then, is to know our sins and our guilt, the sinfulness of our sins and the fearful enormity of our guilt. With the Psalmist in godly sorrow we must confess: "My sins have taken such hold upon me that I am not able to look up;" and with the penitent Prodigal we must cry: "Father, I have sinned before heaven and in Thy sight, and am no more worthy to be called Thy son." We must deeply feel the sense of shame and humiliation. "Tears must be our meat day and night," because of the evil of our hearts; and we must feel a strong and sincere aversion to it, a bitter hatred for it, and a hearty desire to flee from it.

Two pictures must always be before our eyes; the picture of St. Peter, covering his face with his hands and wiping from his furrowed cheeks the hot tears of repentance for having denied his Master; and the picture of the Publican in the Temple, with uplifted hands but down-cast eyes, bringing his unworthiness to God in the prayer, "God, be merciful to me a sinner." That same sorrow which filled St. Peter's heart we, too, must feel; and that prayer of the Publican must not only be on our tongues but in our hearts. You and I must be able to say in truth: That publican, that sinner, am I.

Then, feeling heartfelt sorrow for our sins, and deploring our misdeeds, we must come unto Him who bids all who are "weary and heavy laden" to come to Him that they may find peace. This is the second part of repentance. First, a turning from and a turning against sin with a deep conviction of its terrible consequences upon us and its loathsomeness to God; and next, a turning to God in sorrowful confession, with a prayer for forgiveness of past sins and grace for the future.

It is well that we may come unto Him; that in our sorrows and our sins we have some One to go to—some One to call to our aid. "He has given us rest by His sorrow, and life by His death; rest from our sorrow, from our fear, and from the hard bondage wherein we were made to serve;" and that inward peace which comes only from above. Conscious of our sins, and of our guilt, and of our condemnation, and of our need of forgiveness, here is One who, in the mercy and the compassion of His Heart, brings pardon and grace. Convinced of the corruption of our nature and the depravity of our souls, and of our need of sanctification, here is One who, in love and in kindness, cleanses our nature and purifies our souls. Knowing our subjection to the kingdom of darkness and our need of deliverance from the power of Satan, here is One who, with divine goodness and divine strength, and with the costliest of all gifts, ransoms us. Repentant, and confessing with sorrowful and contrite hearts all our past sins, and our weakness in present dangers and temptations, here is One "who despiseth not the sighing of the contrite nor the desire of such as are sorrowful," but will hear and "save to the uttermost." Repentant and confessing, pardoned, purified, ransomed and saved, the Father from above looks down upon each one of us—upon you and upon me—and sees no longer our sins but His own beloved Son abiding in us; and in that sight He, in infinite mercy, overlooks all that still mars our life, and heeds not the impurities which still cling to us, or the infirmities which still beset us, or the disorder which still remains, or our utter unworthiness to receive His blessing or behold His face. He sees only His well-beloved Son in us, and owns us as one with Him. He loves His own dear Son, and loves us in Him for His sake. And thus, repentant and confessing, pardoned, purified, ransomed and saved, our unrighteousness is forgiven and our sins are covered through the pleading of the One Sacred Heart of the Son, and by the grace and mercy of the Father.

But we are to repent not only because our sins are an abomination to God, and our guilt an accursedness to us, but because "the Kingdom of Heaven is at hand"—nay, "the Kingdom of God is within us;" because "life and immortality have been brought to light," and are in us "the power of God unto salvation." We are even now within the walls of the heavenly city, surrounded by the countless host of pure and spotless beings, "filled with all the fulness of God." Though our minds cannot grasp the thought, and thought cannot compass the truth, yet even now our inner hearts are in some measure, and in a mysterious way, conscious of the strange reality. Christ apprehends us, and we apprehend Christ. We feel ourselves drawn to a whole world of Life. We feel the presence around us of an innumerable company, and within us of a blessed Being blessing us—of a Holy Being making us holy. Forms which cannot be seen are felt by our side; and living as we live, in eternity with God. A host of heavenly beings are guiding us by day and watching over us by night; worshipping God in His Holy Place, and lifting their hands with ours at the Altar; kneeling with us in our closets, and lifting their voices with ours in common prayer and praise. A common life, which knows no bound, is thrilling, as a vast tide, around us and around them, within us and within them. The whole Life of the Incarnation is felt in our hearts, quickening them and filling them with the fulness of blessings, conforming us more and more to the image of Christ, and changing us more and more into creatures of glory. Love embraces, and penetrates, and absorbs us, and knits us, by mystery divine, into one blessed communion with all who are hidden in the Bosom of the Father.

Oh, then, why not repent of our sins, and turn unto the Lord our God while He is near? Why not confess and forsake our sins, that we may have "perfect remission and forgiveness?" Then the Lord will be gracious, and of tender mercy, and will draw us near unto Himself in sweet communion and fellowship here on earth, and nearer still in the Home beyond.

FOURTEENTH DAY OF LENT.

Consciousness of Sin, and Confession of Sin.

God be merciful to me a sinner.—St. Luke xviii. 13.

TWO things are plainly seen in "the publican, who, standing afar off, would not lift up so much as his eyes unto heaven, but smote upon his breast, saying, God be merciful to me a sinner;" two things which must also be found in you and in me and in all who would come unto God. He knew himself a sinner, and he confessed it before God; he was conscious of the evil of his nature, the perverseness of his heart, the sinfulness of his soul, and acknowledged it before Him "who seeth in secret" and seeth into the heart's most secret depths. Not only this, but in the Greek it says, "be merciful to me *the* sinner;" not the sinner in comparison with others, but as showing the extreme depth of intense self-abasement; God be merciful to me, sinner that I am. He left comparisons to the Pharisee, and thought only of his own wicked heart; he felt only his own sinful condition, and his need of mercy and forgiveness.

So must we, you and I, think, and know, and feel, ere we can receive mercy and grace. We must know and feel that we are sinners, great sinners, ere we can know and feel God's mercy and forgiveness. There is nothing, perhaps, that so well shows to us, and to others, our sinfulness as the knowledge of how often we have repented of a sin and then shortly after backslided again; how we have grieved over a sin, and presently sinned again; how we have fought against a temptation, and then fell into it; how we have resolved to lead godly lives, and then broke our resolve; how we took one step forward and then a step—perhaps two steps—backward; how we have prayed for "grace to help in time of need" and then forgot all about it. There is nothing that shows better than this how deeply sinful we are, how fast hold sin has on us, how enslaved we are by it, how much we are under its power. There is nothing that makes us more conscious of the dominion of sin, of the power of darkness, of the terrible antagonism of the soul's enemies, as our frequent defeats and falls. Nor does anything make us more conscious than these do, of our own weakness and powerlessness to meet these evil spirits, to overcome these spiritual enemies, to beat down Satan under our feet, and root out of our heart all weeds of our nature. We may have always believed the great doctrines of the Church—God's love, man's sinfulness, Christ's Atonement, the Spirit's sanctifying work, Heaven and Hell; but we have believed them from afar. They have been no part of us. Even our belief in man's sinfulness has been something vague and distant. We have not come to look away from mankind in its vastness to that little part of it which each of us calls "I;" nor have we left off saying, "man is sinful," and taken up the heart's cry of misery, "I am sinful." But there is nothing that will make us do this, nothing that will make us so conscious of our own sinful condition and our helplessness in sin, as a knowledge of our frequent—our constant—defeats and falls.

This is one of the two things which the publican knew and felt, and which we must know and feel. We must come face to face with our sins, not with sin in the world but with sin in the heart; with the many sins which you and I have committed and do now commit. We must be conscious of them, convinced of them, see them in their true light as deeply hateful to God and eternally hurtful to us. Our sins of omission and sins of commission, our sins of habit and sins of character, the "sin which doth so easily beset us," and the sins which crucify the Son of God afresh, all the sins of our hearts in their myriad forms, we must feel and know as the first step towards mercy and forgiveness. And feel and know them not lightly, but with a recollection that is bitter, that touches the heart and fills us with sorrow and shame, that pains our innermost soul, and drives us to God that He may pluck from the soul their fiery brands. We must deeply feel for ourselves the truth of the Apostle's words: "If we say that we have no sin, we deceive ourselves, and the truth is not in us;" and feel the truth of the prophet's words: "There is none that doeth good, no, not one;" and we must feel that this means us particularly.

Then this first step towards better things will lead to the second. Consciousness of sin will lead to confession of sin. No sooner do we feel ourselves "the sinner," than we say: "God be merciful to me the sinner." No sooner do we find ourselves unclean, than we come to the Fountain for cleansing. No sooner do we feel the disease of the soul, than we come for pardon and healing. This should be our chief desire, as it is our first duty. The Church puts confession of sins the first thing in the service, before ever we utter a word of prayer or praise; so should it also be the first thing in our closet. As in the worship of "the great congregation," so in our devotions in secret and behind closed doors. The Church puts this first because this is the most natural thing to do, and the most honest. When we have done aught against any one, unless we are brazen and hard-hearted, we confess and ask forgivness before we ask another favor. So with ourselves and God. We should, and must, confess our sins for the week, or for the day, before He will turn a listening Ear to our requests. "He is of purer eyes than to behold iniquity," and we must first feel and confess our iniquity, before He will hear our wants and answer according to our need.

It is plain, however, that more is meant by confession of sins than the mere telling them out with the lips. If this were all, God would not require it of us. He knows our sins better than we do. Unto Him "all hearts are open, all desires known, and from Him no secrets are hid;" and He does not need to be told our sins as a mere bit of information. He wants us, then, to confess our sins that we, too, may know them, and know them with godly sorrow; confess them with humbleness of heart, with penitence and full purpose of new obedience and amendment of life. To confess in earnest, then, is to give the cry of the "broken and contrite heart," "God be merciful to me the sinner."

To know and to confess our sins—what a labor of

vast proportions this would be, were we to name each of our sins one by one. "In many things we offend all," says the Apostle. "O Lord our God, other lords besides Thee have had dominion over us," says the prophet. These "other lords" have made the best of their dominion over our hearts, and our offenses are more than can be numbered. Think of all those you and I have committed the past week! And think there have been other weeks with their offences! And think how the weeks roll into months, and the months into years, with a vast number of sins to account for at the end! Think, too, how these sins will once be called up, one by one, to accuse us and condemn us. Will it be well with the soul, do you think, in that day, when our countless sins will be brought forth, like a mighty army; and these "other lords" will come up to claim us as their "peculiar people"—peculiar in the sinfulness of our hearts, in the perverseness of our whole being, in the depravity of our desires and affections?

But we need not name them one by one, nor fear to meet and face them in that awful Day, if now we confess and forsake them, and utter the penitent's cry: "God be merciful to me the sinner." "Perfect love casteth out fear;" and Infinite Love has promised by His Apostle that "if we confess our sins, He is faithful and just to forgive us our sins, and to cleans us from all unrighteousness.

Let us then show this Lent, and all the time henceforth, these two things that are so prominent in the publican and so necessary in us. Let us know ourselves honestly as we are, that knowing our sins we confess them, and in confession find forgivness. Sweet will be the peace that will settle over the heart with God's answer to our penitent cry; sweet the comfort that will come to the soul with our confession and God's pardon. Should we confess to-night as we retire, and this be our last night on earth, still we know that with an honest confession there would come a Voice that would declare all things well. The Lord loveth "mercy and forgiveness, though we have rebelled against Him;" and there is nothing so pleasing to His Ear, nothing that so kindles His love, as the penitent cry, "God be merciful to me the sinner."

FIFTEENTH DAY OF LENT.

Self-Consecration.

I beseech you therefore, brethren, by the mercies of God, that ye present your bodies a living sacrifice, holy, acceptable unto God, which is your reasonable service.—Romans xii. 1.

WITH each celebration of the Holy Eucharist we lift our hearts to God the Father in prayer and say: "Here we offer and present unto Thee, O Lord, ourselves, our souls and bodies, to be a reasonable, holy and living sacrifice unto Thee;" humbly beseeching Him to grant, among other things, that we may "be filled with His grace and heavenly benediction, and made one body with Him, that He may dwell in us and we in Him."

Do we ever stop to think what this means? Do we fully realize what vast and serious things we are praying for in these few words? Think for one moment—and think in all seriousness—there, at God's Holy Altar, in the most solemn act of worship man can engage in, on our knees, while we commemorate the sacrifice of our Lord for us and our salvation, we declare, in words of prayer, that we offer and present ourselves to Him who has offered Himself for us and to us; there, in a most solemn moment and in most solemn stillness, when we closely connect the One Great Sacrifice with our Eucharistic "Sacrifice of praise and thanksgiving," we offer a dedicatory sacrifice of ourselves, our bodies as well as our souls, in living, holy fellowship and indwelling, He in us and we in Him, with all of grace and heavenly benediction that may flow therefrom.

What better thing can we do than to give ourselves wholly to Him who has given Himself wholly to us? How can we better show our appreciation of the wonderful love of God, of the unspeakable pity, of the grace incomprehensible, which has ever followed us into all our sin, to the lowest depth of wickedness wherever we have gone, and has drawn us, striven with us, quickened us, that we may evermore arise to the full purpose of that love and that grace in our hearts! Knowing our sins and our sinfulness, repenting of them, and confessing and forsaking them, what else could we do—you and I—but give ourselves up to God in voluntary self-sacrifice, and in thankful obedience to Him for His mercies in Christ.

Unless we do this the Sacrifice of Christ for us will not only be not complete, but will have no power for us unto salvation. He took up His Cross for us, and we must take up our cross for Him. He laid down His Life for the sheep—and laid it down of Himself—the Creator for the creature—God Incarnate for sinful man—a voluntary Offering; and so likewise should we lay down our lives, dedicate our souls and bodies, surrender our entire selves—our mind, heart, will and affections; all our faculties, all our powers, all parts of our being, all our thoughts, words and deeds, to Him. He gave us all that we may give all back to Him again.

Now, one of the chief reasons, and perhaps the inclusive reason, why we should give ourselves wholly to God, is because "we are buried with Christ by

Baptism into death"—into the death of the old man of sin—"that like as Christ was raised from the dead, even so we should walk in newness of life;" because we are "crucified with Christ," because our "bodies," no less than our souls, "are the temples of the Holy Ghost," and "members of Christ," and "we are not our own," but are "bought with a price."

True religion, then, concerns the body no less than the soul; salvation is for the body as well as the soul. Think, then, how complete a surrender of ourselves we must make; how searchingly God will look for the full measure of self-sacrifice. He will not be satisfied with a half-hearted service. He will not be pleased with an indifferent, listless, lukewarm faith and obedience. He will not be mocked by pretences, and regardeth with anger a worship that is not to His honor and glory.

Too often we think, and act, as if salvation was only for the soul; as if the body would not rise again; as if worship was something spiritual for the soul or the heart only, in which the body could not engage; as if the soul must cleave unto God, but that the body might be given to all sorts of vices without breaking God's Commandments. We live in the world as if soul and body were in no way connected; as if the soul should worship God, but that the body might serve the devil; as if the soul should serve God one day in seven, but that the body might serve Mammon six days in each week. What is such worship and such service but an abomination unto the Lord!

That devotion, that sacrifice, which God calls for, and which will sanctify us, is a full and perfect consecration to the service of God, a complete surrender of our will to His will; and consists in doing His will precisely at the time, in the place, and under the circumstances, to which He has called us. Not only this; but perfect self-consecration demands not only that we do God's will, but that we do it with loving hearts. God desires willing sacrifices. And here we must have Christ for our Pattern. "Lo," said He, "I come to do Thy will, O God." "Not My will," said He, "but Thine be done." His whole life was one great Sacrifice, an unselfing of Himself; from first to last an unselfish devotion to the Father's will. So must we live in continued submission of our will to the Divine will; in doing, bearing and suffering, being led on by the one thought of walking only in the way of the Lord. Having renounced the world, the flesh and the devil, we must resolve to serve none but God alone, and to make it the chief concern of our lives to keep His holy commandments. Having taken solemn vows, which, alas! we have so often violated, we must endeavor by God's help to keep them inviolate to our life's end. As "the children of the flesh are not the children of God," we must crucify the flesh with its affections and lusts." Unable of ourselves to do anything that is good, we must pray God to perfect His strength in our weakness, that our footsteps slip not. Then, conforming our whole life to the Pattern of our Saviour, we will surely find mercy by His merits.

Seeing ourselves as we are—seeing ourselves as God sees us—our heart, our life, our character, secret and open, the depth into which by sin we have fallen, the height from which we have fallen, is God's love not wonderful that He should follow man into such depths of sin; and His mercy that He should, in spite of man's fluctuations, forgive and translate him into the Kingdom of His Dear Son? Yet He "pardoneth iniquity, and passeth by the transgressions of His heritage; He retaineth not His anger forever, because He delighteth in mercy; He will turn again; He will have compassion upon us; He will subdue our iniquities; He will cast all our sins into the depths of the sea."

Then why should we not—you and I—turn unto the Lord our God, and give Him the sacrifice of "ourselves, our souls and bodies," in thankful service for such merciful kindness? What stubborn hearts have we—you and I—what cold and wayward spirits—that we cannot give Him the honor due unto His name! Where are our thoughts that we mind not God who thinketh upon mercy? Oh, let us dedicate ourselves this day anew to His blessed service, in body and in soul, in feeling, thinking, willing and doing, that, He in us and we in Him, we may have peace in ourselves and unbroken union with God.

SIXTEENTH DAY OF LENT.

"Have mercy on me."

And he cried, saying, Jesus, thou Son of David, have mercy on me.—St. Luke xviii. 38.

WE all know the story. They were on their way to Jerusalem — Christ and the disciples. He told them how that all that was written of Him should be fulfilled; how He should be betrayed and delivered into the hands of His enemies; how He should be mocked and scourged and spitefully entreated, and put to death. He told them how He must suffer for the many — the Just for the unjust — that the prophecies might be fulfilled, and the unjust many might be justified and saved.

On the way they pass by a blind beggar. Astonished at the unusual din of men's voices, and the strange sayings, the beggar asks: "What means this tumult?" Told that it is the Lord and Master, with His disciples, he beseeches the Lord's blessing, and prays that he may receive sight. Behold! it is done.

The blind man is a poor man; poor in worldly goods and possessions, poor in bodily health and strength; sick, sore, blind, infirm, tottering, helpless, distressed, he is, to all appearances, a miserable and pitiable portion of humanity. He presented a sad picture, indeed. He had no home, no friends, no care such as a poor, blind and helpless man should have.

Left to take care of himself as best he could, he roamed from city to city, and sat by the wayside begging. Whatever compassion the passers-by might have on him, was all the cheer and comfort he had in this world.

Beloved, is this not a picture of us all? Are we not all in spiritual poverty and nakedness, blind of heart and sick of soul, entirely helpless under the powerful dominion of Satan and sin? Are we not all—you and I—blind to all the signs of God's goodness; deaf to all the voices by which He speaks to our hearts; and dumb when we should have upon our lips the accents of prayer, or praise, or thanksgiving? They that went with Christ rebuked the blind man, that he should hold his peace; and the multitudes that follow us—legions of evil spirits—beg us be still and let our Saviour pass by. Those sins, small and great, secret and open, that have taken such hold upon us, that beset us before and behind, cast their poisonous influence over our hearts and our consciences, bidding us stifle every cry for mercy and help from our merciful Lord, hoping that they may, a while longer, reign supreme in our hearts and feast upon our souls. And, alas! too often the evil spirits have their own way; and Christ, who may have stopped to hear and help us, passes by in silence and in sorrow.

Therefore, let us learn a lesson from the blind beggar. He knew his infirmities, and sought relief from the Great Physician, Healer of souls and bodies. He knew his sins and shortcomings, and sought forgiveness and redemption. He knew his poverty of worldly goods, and sought the unbounded wealth of the heavenly. He was without earthly friends, and sought Him who is the "Friend indeed." In his dire extremity he called for help, and was helped. Disregarding the rebukes of the multitude, who would have deprived him of the consolation he so much craved, he continued his cry: "Son of David, have mercy on me." So should, and so must we—you and I—if we wish to be helped. The beggar's idea of Christ must be our idea; and our entreaties must be as earnest as his. Would God we were blind, then should we also see—blind to the world, to the flesh, to the Devil; blind to all that leads us away from Christ—then should we see our sins, and see the glory of Christ and of His Cross that covers all sin. The pleasures of the world now cloud our eyes, that we see not the infinitely more pleasant things of God. Our worldly-mindedness hides from our eyes the love, the mercy, and the grace of our Saviour. We are continually occupied with such things as profit nothing to the soul; and only a moment is devoted to the work of our salvation. What if we do busy ourselves with this world's goods?—is the world gained, there is nothing gained; but, is the soul lost, all is lost. Would, then, that we had the blindness of this wayside beggar, then we might see our faults and follies, our sins and shortcomings, our misery and wretchedness, and cry for spiritual sight—that sight which comes of a pure heart. Then, indeed, would the Kingdom of God be nigh at hand—nay, within our souls.

How often do we need mercy! Never a day but we need the strong arm of our Lord to overcome Satan; or His grace to withstand temptation. Even then, we frequently fall, because we have not that steadfast faith which is so necessary in all the assaults of evil. We are prone to all evil, and backward to all good; and we need mercy all the day long. Then let this prayer for mercy be on our lips all the day long: "Have mercy on me, O God, after Thy great goodness;" and the Lord, out of the great goodness of His great Heart, will have mercy, and forgive. Then we will learn how true are the prophet's words: "How great is the loving-kindness of the Lord our God, and His compassion unto such as turn unto Him in holiness."

> "Have mercy, Lord, on me,
>   As Thou wert ever kind;
> Let me, oppress'd with loads of guilt,
>   Thy wonted mercy find.
>
> "Wash off my foul offence,
>   And cleanse me from my sin;
> For I confess my crime, and see
>   How great my guilt has been.
>
> "Blot out my crying sin,
>   Nor me in anger view;
> Create in me a heart that's clean,
>   An upright mind renew.
>
> "Withdraw not Thou Thy help,
>   Nor cast me from Thy sight;
> Nor let Thy Holy Spirit take
>   His everlasting flight.
>
> "Have mercy, Lord, on me,
>   As Thou wert ever kind;
> Let me, oppress'd with loads of sin,
>   Thy wonted mercy find."

Yea, conscious of those sins whereof our conscience is afraid, and of those offences of lip and heart which we constantly commit, let our constant cry be: "Son of David, have mercy on me." And then, in the clouds will appear the sunshine; and in the stillness will come a Voice—a sweet, low, soft, tender Voice—full of sympathy, and love, and blessing; and o'er the heart will steal a peace that passeth understanding—the peace of God—the peace of mercy and forgiveness.

SEVENTEENTH DAY OF LENT.

THE SINNER'S FRIEND.

A friend of publicans and sinners.—St. Matthew xi. 19.

THESE words were not spoken with any intention to please or compliment. They were not meant to discribe with admiration the character of Christ. They were not spoken by one who would, under any circumstances, have complimented Him. They were spoken in scornful and contemptuous mood, and by an enemy; like many other things that were said of Him, that spoke truth but were not meant to do Him credit,—like the charge, "this man receiveth sinners and eateth with them," and like the inscription on the Cross. Yet what was meant as a reproach has come to be an honor; what was a reflection upon His character has come to be a source of happiness to us who are His people.

Who is a sinner, and how is Christ the Friend of sinners? Let us look for a while at these two questions that grow out of our text.

Who is a sinner? If we are honest when this question is put, we are each of us thinking of ourselves. We do not ask, am I a sinner? but we say, I am a sinner, I am the sinner. We feel the infection of sin in us, and in all; we see it working in us, and in all; so that "if we say," or any one says, "that we have no sin, we deceive ourselves, and the truth is not in us." Not only so, but the guilt and condemnation of sin is upon us all. We feel a load of iniquity. We feel the burden of good things left undone, and of evil things which we have done. We feel the weakness of our flesh in doing that which we ought to do, and an inclination to do that which we ought not to do. We know and feel our sins against light and conviction, against warnings and mercies; while we have sinned, and sinned, and sinned again, and loved to sin, notwithstanding our better knowledge and the protests of our conscience. And we know and feel our sins of ignorance by the marks they have left upon us, the weakness they have left us in, the increasing inclination to sin, the increasing feebleness of conscience. Sin is the fatal disease of our souls; the plague of our hearts, the blight of our lives, most malignant and desperate. We are conscious of its presence in our thoughts; we see it in the words of our mouths and the meditations of our hearts; we feel it working towards the ends of our fingers to do that which we ought not; and bidding our feet to walk in paths that are forbidden. There is scarce a moment of our wakeful lives, when it does not lift its head to do that which is amiss. "All have sinned." "All we like sheep have gone astray." "There is none that doeth good, no, not one." All are sinners. In our trials innumerable, we sorely feel the need of a Friend; in our sorrows and distresses we feel the need of a Comforter; in our humiliating defeats and falls, we feel the need of a strong arm able and willing to help and defend. In our darkest hour, in our gloomiest prospects, in the slough of despair, even though fallen and outcast, we are here made to look on One who is the Friend of publicans and sinners; and made to look to Him as our Helper and Defender; One who has offered Himself to sinners and not to the righteous, to the sick and not to them that need not a physician; One whose whole earthly life was spent among sinners and for their everlasting good; whose every thought was upon them and their needs; whose every word was uttered in their behalf, calling them to repentance, and teaching them sound doctrine. In Doctrine and Life, by words and works, He proved Himself pre-eminently the "friend of publicans and sinners."

Let us see how He is this more particularly.

In the first place and decidedly not, as many among us are friends of sinners, by aiding and abetting sinners in their wicked deeds; not by participating in their vices and crimes; not by pointing out new paths of sin and following with them these forbidden paths to the end, in wilful forgetfulness of duty and in delight of the evil. Not so was He the sinner's Friend, and not so is He now.

Nor is He the sinner's Friend by merely offering wholesome counsel and sound advice; by holding them at arm's length as if association were contamination; by looking down on them with pity but with dignified courtesy, and pointing them to the way wherein they should go. Not this sort of a Friend was He any more than He was the other. This would not have inspired the love of sinners; nor would the other have left Him sinless. This would not have shown His love for sinners; and the other would have shown His love for sin. He is the sinner's Friend in a far different sense, and in a far higher degree.

The purpose of His coming into the world reveals most clearly the nature of His friendship and its surpassing value. Though "He came unto His own and His own received Him not," He came into the world "that the world through Him might be saved." "The Father sent the Son to be the Saviour of the world." He not only left the highest seat of power and honor in Heaven—yea, the Throne of Heaven, but He stooped to the lowest level of sinful man, that He might, as Man, know their perplexities and wants; feel their lot and station; sympathize with them in their hopes, and fears, and trials, and difficulties, and dangers; give them help in time of need; and save to the uttermost, even with the gift of pardon for their sins and life eternal, all them that come unto Him in repentance and faith.

In this spirit He entered upon His Ministry; in this spirit He wrought miracles of wonder and of healing; in this spirit He taught the multitudes that came unto Him. Most of His miracles show the tenderness and warmth of His Heart towards sorrowing or suffering man; all His Parables show the tenderness and love of His Soul for the people who sit in darkness; both His miracles and parables show the message He bore to the hearts of sinful men—the message of mercy, of grace, of pardon, of love; both show the fulness of His Heart toward publicans and sinners, and the longing of the Father to release them from those bonds that hold and oppress them, and to give them the liberty of life Divine. He ate with publicans and sinners, no house being too humble to give Him shelter; no table too frugally spread to satisfy His desire. His Apostles were selected not from the wealthy and influential Pharisees and the learned Scribes, but from the poor, ignorant Galilean fishermen. He never shunned the company of any who had need of Him, nor excluded Himself from any to whom He could be of service. The application of the needy, the bitter cry of the sorrowful, the penitent and believing prayer of the sinful, never met with repulse. So full of good words and good deeds was He that, even in His last and most agonizing moments, His last words for His enemies were a prayer for their forgivness.

And, as with Him on earth, so with Him in Heaven. As in the days of His humiliation, so in His exaltation. He is still "touched with the feeling of our infirmities;" and, because He hath entered into the Most Holy Place with the Blood of Atonement, He is still more powerful to save. Bearing the whole burden of human sin, feeling the weight of human guilt, and knowing our weakness and inability to do that which is right, He is now more than ever our Intercessor and Advocate—the Friend of publicans and sinners.

All have sinned, and so He is the Friend of all. None are left out. His friendship is as all-embracing as sin is from which He longs to deliver us. None are excluded from His mercy, from His grace, from His pardon, from His love, from His everlasting life, except those who exclude themselves. He will be your Friend, He will be mine, if we will let Him; your Intercessor and mine, if we will not, like the Gadarene herdsmen, pray Him to go out of our coasts, preferring our swine to our Saviour. He is ever accessible, ever near, ever present, ever gracious, compassionate and forgiving; His Ear is ever open and listening for the cry of publicans and sinners; His Heart ever longing for their loving service. Let us, then, in our helplessness look to Him for help; in our temptations look to Him for succor; in our sins look to Him for pardon and grace.

EIGHTEENTH DAY OF LENT.

Jesus our High Priest.

We have not an High Priest which cannot be touched with the feeling of our infirmities; but was in all points tempted like as we are, yet without sin.—Hebrews iv. 15.

HOW can One who is sinless sympathize with sinners? How can He look with any feeling other than anger upon sin? How can He enter into our sorrows, and know that pain, and anguish, and shame, and remorse, and self-abhorrence which come with sin? He has no consciousness of sin; He had no taste of its bitterness; He felt not the piercing shafts of guilt, and wept not the hot tears of repentance. How can He, then, be touched with the feeling of these our greatest infirmities? He and the Prince of this world, His Spirit and the spirit of evil, had nothing in common. He was "holy, harmless, undefiled, separate from sinners." How can He, then, know and understand, and feel in His own soul what sin is to us — what its power, its sting, its guilt? It seems to us impossible; but seems so only because it is a mystery.

He who is pure and holy, and full of fear of even so much as the least sullying thought; who walks with God, clothed even now in the saintly whiteness; who feels the love of God shed abroad in his heart, and whose soul lives in the stillness of eternal peace;

who knows the power of God's mercy, and forgiveness, and grace, and help; who values and treasures his sonship and fellowship with God; he it is who can feel for and sympathize with one who has fallen. His sense of all the good he enjoys, his participation in holiness, makes him deeply sensible of that which the fallen creature lacks or has lost; and his heart goes out to the sinner in pity, sorrow, and sympathy and compassion.

So it is with Christ. His own purity and holiness is the source of all His pity and compassion for sinners. Sin cannot condemn sin, and sinners cannot judge sinners. He alone can judge sin; He alone can attemper justice and mercy to the weakness and frailty of man, who, though He felt the power of temptation in all its might, came scathless through the trial, pure and holy in His mind and heart. And it was by that bitter temptation that He learned the power of sin, and was "touched with the feeling of our infirmities." It was not only as Man, but as being "tempted like as we are," and feeling in His own human Body all its fearful susceptibility of temptation and sin, that He "knoweth our frame, and remembereth that we are but dust."

Nay, more than this, still. It was not merely by His perfect holiness, and His knowledge of us gained by experience with us in our sins; but it was also by His own bitter experience with "the wages of sin," that He knoweth our infirmities and pitieth us. He was despised and rejected of men. "He bore our griefs and carried our sorrows." "He was wounded for our transgressions, and was bruised for our iniquities." In these experiences, and in His last mortal agonies, "He was made perfect through suffering." "He bore our sins in His own Body on the Tree." And by these He knew the power and the guilt of sin; by these He was touched with the feeling of our infirmities;" and by these He was moved, as our "Great High Priest," to offer Himself to God, the propitiatory Sacrifice for the world's stupendous guilt.

He offered Himself to God as Man. Man had sinned, and man had to make reparation for sin. So He became Man, and represented humanity, both in its perfected state and in its fulfilled relations with God. As Man He was so much part of ourselves that all that He was, and suffered, and did was our own, and ourselves in Him doing, and suffering, and sacrificing, and atoning. All that He was He imparts to each one of us in its fullest spirit and power. All that He did He did as Man identified with each one of us. As "without shedding of blood there is no remission," so He "offered sacrifice" for sin—Himself, yet each one of us in Him. As a faithful High Priest He "died unto sin once;" and as a faithful High Priest He "ever liveth to make intercession for us."

It is this that forces from Him, for each one of us, that separate, special discriminating love. It is this —"touched with the feeling of our infirmities"—that makes the Eternal Bosom heave with sorrow for our misdeeds; and that brings to us, from His "Everlasting Arms," "grace to help in time of need." It is this that moves Him to call us to repentance; to invite us to the love-feast; to speak to us words of comfort, and grace, and blessing. It is this that makes Him love the sinner, though He hates the sin. And it is this, too—this love and sympathy for us in our infirmities and sins, "knowing whereof we are made,"—that makes Him the "merciful and faithful High Priest in things pertaining to God, to make reconciliation for the sins of the people."

What a blessed truth, a blessed fact, is stored up in that word "reconciliation," for us and all men in their sins and infirmities! By the exercise of His Priestly Office we are now reconciled to God, and God to us. God is no longer an angry God, but a loving Father; and we are His own well-beloved children. What the High Priest was to Israel on the Day of Atonement, that Christ is to His Church; and all the blessings covenanted in Him, the fulness of blessing "received of the Father," are ours on our becoming His. By the exercise of His Priestly Office He has "redeemed transgressions," and won for us an "eternal inheritance." In the exercise of His Priestly Office He (and we in Him) have passed within the veil—He has entered the Holy of Holies above—and there "continueth now" the Mediator of a new covenant," our "Intercessor and Advocate." By the exercise of His Priestly Office He applies to us—to our hearts, our souls, our nature—the Blood of "the Lamb that was slain," and washes away our confessed and forsaken sins—yours and mine. On the Throne of Heaven He (and we in Him) ask, "with authority," for mercy and pardon, for compassion and grace; and intercedes (He, and we in Him) with the Five Wounds in His Body, with the Blood of the Everlasting Covenant, for forgiveness of our sins and restoration to God's favor and blessing.

But is this all? Are we to rely entirely on His

Priestly Office, and trust to God's mercy for pardon? No. We ourselves have a work to do, an offering to make. We must go to Him who first came to us, and place ourselves in penitence at His feet. We must uncover our shame with honest and contrite hearts. We must fall to the earth with the publican's prayer: "God be merciful to me a sinner." Or, if words fail us, abase ourselves in silence, and let our silence appeal to the sympathies of Him who, in the garden, "fell on His face" under the burden of our infirmities. Heavy is the load, oppressive the burden, of our sins—your sins and mine, and the sins of the whole world from Adam until now. Yet He patiently bore it all then, and He willingly forgives it all now. While we would not so much as lift our eyes unto heaven, but bitterly denounce and condemn ourselves, His Face is lifted up in pity and forgiveness upon us. While in bitterness of soul we chastise ourselves, His peace sinks down into our afflicted hearts. When, in heavy hours and mournful days, in bewilderment of heart and remorse; "when our hearts are smitten down within us, and withered like grass;" when, repentant and confessing, we bend before Him in secret indignation and shame for our sins, His consolation and grace will distil upon our hearts as the dews of early morning wet the thirsty plant. Then that Blood, which is the true Covenant—the Blood of our "merciful and faithful High Priest," which alone can wash the soul of every foul spot—will "cleanse us from all unrighteousness."

NINETEENTH DAY OF LENT.

JESUS THE GOOD SHEPHERD.

I am the Good Shepherd.—St. John x. 11.

THE bigoted, tyrannical, and cruel conduct of the Pharisees toward one who was cured of his blindness and then confessed Christ as a Prophet, caused Christ to draw a parallel between them and Himself, and to contrast, in sharpest lines, their work and motives with His work and motives. They were blind guides, false and hypocritical shepherds; He was the true and sincere Shepherd of the flock, and "the Light of the world."

This gave us one of the most beautiful and affecting allegories found in the Bible, or in any literature; and is called the Parable of the Good Shepherd. So well does it teach the work of Christ, and His devotion to it, and so well is it fitted to inspire us with love for Him, and obedience to Him, that the Church has appointed it to be read, in whole or in part, five times during the year.

Christ calls Himself not only the Shepherd, but, in comparison with the Pharisees, the Good Shepherd;—good in all the things which are characteristic of a faithful shepherd. He cares for us, His sheep; feeds us; and, as is often necessary in a shepherd's efforts to save his sheep from death, He died for us.

He cares for us. He is watching and guarding us incessantly. He bring us by paths we do not know;

makes crooked ways straight, and darkness light before us; never leaves us, and never forsakes us. The way may often be full of thorns and briars; there may be many anxious cares and perplexities. But He beats down the thorns and briars, so that we may go without harm or hurt; He takes our cares upon Himself, and solves for us our perplexities, so that we may possess our souls in peace. If the way through which we must go is narrow, He goes before and selects the best places for us to step; if it leads beside a precipice, and there is danger of falling, He gives us a greater measure of His grace, and leads us more tenderly and carefully; for He is not willing that any should perish, but that all should have life, and should have it more abundantly. If we are footsore, wounded, or sick, He carries us on His shoulder, and binds up our bleeding wounds. Thus, in all our sins and shortcomings, He is more than Good Shepherd, because, besides giving us His tenderest help, He gives us of His grace and Spirit, to withstand and overcome temptations and assaults, to bear the load that wearies us, to resign ourselves to the cares from which we cannot flee, and to carry the griefs and sorrows which we cannot tell, but which He knows so well.

He also feeds us. "He maketh us to lie down in green pastures; He leadeth us beside the still waters. He prepares a table before us in the presence of our enemies;" and "in all the changes and chances of this mortal life," in the Shepherd's keeping we can lack nothing. If the best pastures lie beyond the mountains of trial and across the deserts of grief, where thorns pierce the body and sharp stones bruise the feet, and the sultry sun pours down a perilous heat; or if our path lie past the cane where the howling of bears is heard, or past the thicket where the wolf lies in wait; yet He will lead, guard and defend from evil solicitations, afflictions of body and distress of mind; He will comfort and succour, and make the feast all the more bounteous and taste all the sweeter. He feeds us not alone with earthly food. There is greater and better that He gives us, and gives with a lavish hand, and out of the abundance of His store—Manna from Heaven, Food of Angels, Bread of Life, His own dear Body, and His own precious Blood. In the Sacrament of the Altar He gives us what we have not that is good. He shows us the secrets of His Heart's Love, and gives us spiritual nourishment and refreshment, pardon and grace and life—His Life. Eating this Divine Food more and more, His Life flows into our life more and more; our poor life is enriched; our weak life is strengthened; our sinful life is sanctified. Then we have life, indeed—eternal life; for, "he that eateth of this Bread shall live forever."

Yet, He also died for us. Such was His devotion to His Shepherd-Office, such His Love for His sheep— wandering, erring, rebellious, sinful sheep—that He "laid down His Life for the sheep." Often a shepherd carries his life in his own hands in the care and defence of his flock. Thieves, and wolves, and precipices imperil him as much as they do his sheep; and often, in braving these dangers for his sheep, he loses his own life. So the Good Shepherd, who, from all eternity, was most blessed, abiding with the Father, in the unity of the Holy Ghost, in glory unspeakable, yet in His pure and unspotted Heart had sympathy with us in our extreme suffering by reason of sin; in His most Holy Spirit He tasted the bitterness of sin and endured its burden; and yielded up Himself to be overshadowed, as with a horror of great darkness, that we might be brought to light, and might be saved from our sins and live. For us, He was bruised and spitted on, mocked and despised; for us, He was bowed down with grief and convulsed with the pangs of bitter pain; for us, "He endured the Cross, despising the shame." "Greater love hath no man than this, that a man lay down his life for his friends." And He, who "had power to lay it down and to take it again," gave up His Life, in voluntary and loving sacrifice, for the sins of His people—for your sins and mine—for you and for me.

Thus the shepherd cares for, feeds, and, if necessary, will die for, his sheep. All this the Good Shepherd does, or has done, for us. For this devoted attachment of the shepherd for his sheep, the sheep will form an attachment for the shepherd. They not only know him, but "know his voice;" will hear, and obey, and follow, and trust him. Wherever he leads, they will follow; whatever he requires of them, they will do. This same devotion, this love and obedience, the Good Shepherd expects from us, His sheep—once His lost sheep—for whom He endured and suffered so much.

But, alas! He often expects in vain. We do not love as we should. We do not obey as we ought. He speaks, but we do not hear. He calls, but we give no heed. He leads, but we do not follow. He commands, but we do not obey. He succours us, but we remain ungrateful. He loves us, but we are indifferent and cold. We prefer the plain to the sheepfold, though we see the lion ready to devour us. We prefer the thicket to the safe enclosure, though we hear wild beasts in every direction, which will prey upon us. In the foolishness and perverseness of our hearts, we leave the Shepherd and the pastures He provides, and go to what we think are greener and better pastures and purer and sweeter waters, regardless of the many dangers and temptations with which our way is beset. We want more worldliness than is consistent with our Christian profession. Self-will, evil tempers, fierce passions possess us, and we thereby quench the Spirit and "crucify the Son of God afresh and put Him to an open shame." Worldly cares, worldly company, worldly pleasures, evil pursuits, "the lust of the flesh, the lust of the eye, and the pride of life," all tempt us away from the Shepherd and the flock, from the Divine blessings and the Divine care; and we go on in the world, to the end of our course, and are lost.

Let us give up self-will, curb our tempers, govern our passions, forsake all worldliness, as by our Christian profession we are bound to do; and live only, trustfully and obediently, in the fold of our Divine Shepherd. Then "His rod and His staff shall comfort us," and "goodness and mercy shall follow us all the days of our life, and we will dwell in the house of the Lord forever."

TWENTIETH DAY OF LENT.

JESUS AT THE DOOR.

Behold, I stand at the door, and knock.—Revelation iii. 20.

OUR Lord comes to us in various ways, and often. But far too often we either see Him not, or know Him not, or, knowing Him, refuse Him entrance or slight Him entirely. Every event in our lives which has a marked character, every turning point, every illness or affliction, every great loss or heavy disappointment or bitter bereavement, brings Christ to us with a message of better things to come. In all our blighted hopes, in all our thwarted wishes, in all that darkens our path or clouds our souls, Christ comes with a surer hope and a truer happiness. In every stirring of conscience, and every serious thought; in sudden visitations and in the whispering of the wind; in the pursuit of pleasure or sin by day, and in the quiet hour of the night, Christ comes to us and speaks of repentance and self-consecration, of a life of godliness and a life everlasting. When we live away from God He comes to us and asks, as He asked Adam, "Where art thou?" When we are helplessly under the dominion of sin, He pleads with us as Moses pleaded with his father-in-law, saying: "Come thou with us and we will do thee good." In all our losses and disappointments He comes and speaks of a "better part which shall not be taken away from us," "an inheritance incorruptible, and undefiled, and that fadeth not away."

He comes to us also in the preaching of His Word, and in the administration of His Sacraments; in holy days and holy seasons, when we commemorate "the mystery of His holy Incarnation," or His "holy Nativity" or "Circumcision," His "Baptism, Fasting, and Temptation," His "Agony and Bloody Sweat," "His Cross and Passion, precious Death and Burial, glorious Resurrection and Ascension," and "the coming of the Holy Ghost;" in all these He comes to all of us—to each one of us—to you and to me—with a message of love and mercy, grace and forgiveness, of repentance and faith and obedience.

But alas! for the hardness of our hearts, and the sinfulness of our souls, we will not look up and behold His coming; we will not hear His knocking; we will not open the door that He may enter in. He stands without in patience and meekness, and knocks, and knocks, and knocks, but we are never so deaf as when He asks to come into our hearts. Hear Him say as He stands there and knocks: "If any man hear My voice, and open the door, I will come in to him and will sup with him and he with Me," and "My Father will love him and We will come unto Him and make Our abode with him;" "I will not leave you comfortless." Yet we hear Him not. He will sup with us and we with Him, and will not leave us comfortless; not only He, but the Father also will abide with us, and abide forever, if we will let Him; but these inducements are nothing compared with those attractions of "the world, the flesh, and the devil" to which we seem bound as it were by adamantine chains. We want Him not yet, we want none of His blessings, great and good though we know them to be; but we want them not yet. A little more of the world, of worldly pleasures, of the worship of Mammon; a little more of this, and of that, though they are corruptible as the beasts that perish. A little more of "the earth, earthy," and then all of heaven; a little more of time and temporal pursuits, and then a thought upon eternity and eternal things. We have no time now for things so distant and future.

No wonder He comes to us, and knocks, and desires to come into our hearts. Such hearts most need His coming. Hearts so worldly, souls so sinful, as those that have no thought of God and eternity, surely most need the Saviour's coming. Look at our hearts—yours and mine. Are they swept and garnished, or do seven other spirits more wicked than before inhabit them? Look no further than the door, see where Christ now stands, see what meets His Eye as He stands there and knocks. See the grass and weeds that fill the path which leads to our hearts, over which Christ had to come to get to our hearts. See the briars and vines that are trailing wildly over the door. See all the rank growths that pain His Eye, and indicate the desolation and poverty of soul within—that indicate our sins and evils, our faults and shortcomings. Long neglect of our hearts has filled them, and covered them within and without, with the wild and bitter fruits of wickedness. And now Christ stands at the door and knocks, wishing to be let in, wishing to drive out these evil spirits, wishing to cleanse and purify and sanctify our hearts, and to make them His dwelling-place, and temples of the Holy Spirit, forever.

He knocks loud and long. Again and again He knocks. He looks tired as He stands there waiting to be let in; sad and anxious, careworn, expectant and wondering—expecting to enter in and wondering why we do not open. That look of hope which filled His Eye when He first came has left, and He is now down-cast and disappointed. You can see by the deep lines on His Brow, by His bent Form and His slow step, that He has gone through much suffering, a sorrow even unto death. We see a crown of thorns encircling His Brow, and Blood flowing where the sharp prongs pierced His Flesh. As He looks up you may see tears on His Cheeks, tears of sorrow and anguish for the sins of His people. You may see the expression on His Face grow more sad and His Eyes more tearful as He is kept waiting. Now and then you may hear Him say: "Behold, I stand at the door and knock; if any man hear My voice, and open the door, I will come in to him, and sup with him and he with Me." But he is kept knocking and waiting and waiting and knocking. Either we hear Him not for the noise inside, or our business and cares preoccupy us so that we heed nothing besides.

As He knocks we see a wound in His Hand—a wound in each Hand, and in His Feet, and His Side; and we hear the Prophet saying unto us: "He was wounded for our transgressions, He was bruised for our iniquities, the chastisement of our peace was upon Him." For you and for me was He wounded and bruised, for your transgressions and iniquities and mine; yet He knocks, but we will not hear; He speaks but we will not listen; He shows us His wounds but we are not touched; He would comfort us and sup with us, but we will not open.

And what is that supping with Him and with the Father of which He speaks? It is the fulness of heavenly blessings, "the fulness of God." It is grace and mercy, and pardon and peace. It is kindness and love and hope and strength. It is life and holiness and sanctification and redemption,—immortality in which all other blessings are gathered and towards which all others tend. All that His Love can accomplish in us, all that His Heart can bestow, He will give us, if we will hear His Voice and let Him enter our hearts.

There are many who will never hear and never open. He knocks again and again, and listens for the footsteps of the one within to come and let Him in; but no. He must turn away and go; and as He goes we hear Him say: "They will not come to Me that they might have life." "If thou hadst known, even thou, at least in this thy day, the things which belong unto thy peace; but now they are hid from thine eyes." That soul wants not Christ, and Christ cannot bless him. As in the days of His Flesh, so often even now, "He comes unto His own, but His own receives Him not."

Can it be possible that there is one among us who keeps Christ knocking and waiting, who will not let Him in? Nay, rather let me believe that we are all faithful disciples of our Lord. Poor as we are, let me think that we are all "rich in faith" and in redemption. Wretched as we are, let me think that we are all made clean in the Blood of the Lamb. Weak, sinful and unworthy, as all men are, let me think that our hearts are all lit up with the smile of a Divine Guest; and that our souls are furnished with the goodly adornments of the saints in light. In want as we are, and as all men are, let me think that there is One abiding with us, who provides, out of His abundant store, that "hidden Manna" which nourishes life everlasting; and that there is One supping with us and we with Him, whose presence is fulness of joy for evermore.

TWENTY-FIRST DAY OF LENT.

Jesus the Water of Life.

If any man thirst, let him come unto Me, and drink.—St. John vii. 37.

Whosoever drinketh of the water that I shall give him shall never thirst; but the water that I shall give him shall be in him a well of water springing up into everlasting life.—St. John iv. 14.

CHRIST and His disciples had come a distance of twenty miles, in the sultry heat and dust; and now, towards evening, they were at the well of Sychar, foot-sore, weary and hungry. While the greater number of disciples were in the town to buy food that all might eat, the Samaritan woman came to the well to draw water. It was the well which our Lord's great ancestor, and the ancestor of all Israel, had digged; the well also where was the first rebellion against God's order, against the Davidic line and against the Temple. Here then surely was a place where Christ's Heart, full of sadness because of His expulsion from the Temple and the Holy City, would yearn for the love of all God's people, and think of the breach and of what alone could heal it. Forgetful of His own hunger of Body, He thought far more of that spiritual hunger and thirst, and of that Meat and Drink which is the Food of the soul. By the side of this ancient well, weary and thirsty, He thought of that other Well, and its water of life, of which whosoever drinketh shall never thirst again;

water of everlasting life, given in unfailing supply and unending refreshment.

But she, who was the occasion of this beautiful doctrine, was a Samaritaness, poor, ignorant, and of low birth and character; and the Israelite has no dealings with the Samaritan other than necessity requires. Her surprise can therefore be imagined when, on coming to the well where Christ sat, she heard Him not only ask for a drink, but enter into conversation with her.

This very fact, if she gave any thought at all to it, taught her that the Man before her was no ordinary man such as she saw every day. He was not a Jew like those she had hitherto known; not like what she had hitherto thought them to be. Even with this first request, "Give Me to drink," with the tenderness of His voice, the friendliness of His bearing, and the interest He took in her, she learned that there was something about the Man she had never before seen or known; but what the difference was she could not yet see.

But Christ did not leave her in suspense. He unfolded to her the history of her life, both open and secret, all things that ever she did; and proved to the astonished woman that He was a Prophet. It was a revelation of Himself to her, no less than a revelation of her past life. Was this indeed that Prophet promised by Moses, and foretold by the other prophets? Was she not beholding the long-expected Messiah? Was she not, perhaps, in the presence of the Omniscient One Himself? Yes, a prophet and more than a prophet, the Messiah, the Omniscient One in very truth; the Lord and Giver of

Life; for whosoever shall drink of the water which He will give shall never thirst, but it shall spring up in him into everlasting life.

Thus the greatest boon came to the woman out of infinite condescension and grace. Christ approached her with unrestrained freedom, allowed no barriers to stand in the way of doing good; but seeing the spiritual ignorance and destitution of this woman, He breathed into her soul the breath of a life that is eternal. He indeed asked of her a favor, but only that He might grant an infinitely greater favor in return. He drank of her water, but gave in unmeasured abundance the water of life to her who ministered to Him. She, too, stood beside a Well; the perennial fountain of life, purity, goodness, peace, and happiness. She stood spiritually foot-sore, weary, and parched; but as He quenched His earthly thirst with her earthly water, so she drank of the water which He alone can give, and quenched her thirst forever.

Her material thirst is but a figure of that ever deeper spiritual thirst which you and I and all mortals feel or have felt at some period of our lives; ever deeper and ever deepening, because contact with evil and sin quickens to intensity our need and our desire for a quenching of that thirst. As our natural and worldly desires are never satisfied by earthly possessions, much less can our yearning of soul be. These reach out after God, and eternity, and heavenly beatitudes; and these are fully met and satisfied by the revelation of pardon and love in Christ, so that with one full draught of the living water which flows from Him, the soul shall never thirst. The listening heart of the woman began to perceive the glorious end of the Master's teaching, and her eyes began to fill with visions of unfading realities, as she "drew water out of the Well of salvation." So will we and all "who hunger and thirst after righteousness," be filled and refreshed and satisfied, if we obey the voice of Christ, calling in the Temple, "If any man thirst, let him come unto Me and drink." Washed clean from all stains of sin will not only be each thirsty heart that drinks of this fountain, but with the stream of living water will flow into each heart His manifold mercies and abundant grace. Each mortal breast pants far and wide for these water-brooks, though many, perhaps, all unknowing. Each seeks with a longing far from gratified the happiness found in Him, as the new-mown hay thirsts for the dew of even; and only with His sprinkling, or with His washing, or with His cup of living water will the faint heart or the parched tongue revive.

"There is a fountain opened for all uncleanliness;" and to all, to you and to me, comes the voice of the prophet, crying: "Ho, every one that thirsteth, come ye to the waters;" a Fountain that shall "purge the conscience from dead works to serve the living God;" a Fountain that shall purify and cleanse the soul, and yet also forever meet all its inward wants; yea, a Fountain that shall not only quench the thirst forever of him that drinks, but shall spring up in him into everlasting life. It is a Fountain of love and forgiveness, of consolation and peace, of mercy and grace not only here, but of increasing abundance of the gifts of God hereafter; whose source is both in the love that spared not His own Son, and in the Heart of the Son who offered Himself for us, and whose final issue is in the salvation of all who are defiled by sin.

Do we, you and I, feel this water of life welling up in our hearts? Do we all feel our souls washed with the pure water that flows out of the fountain opened for sin in the Heart of Christ? This cleansing and healing water is ever flowing out of the Well of everlasting life; and to us in our sins and shortcomings, "the Spirit and the Bride say, Come,—and let him that heareth say, Come,—and let him that is athirst come,—and whosoever will, let him take the water of life freely."

God grant us all this washing and this draught of living water; and grace ever to keep ourselves pure and unspotted from the world.

TWENTY-SECOND DAY OF LENT.

Jesus the True Vine.

I am the Vine, ye are the branches: He that abideth in Me, and I in him, the same bringeth forth much fruit; for without Me (or, severed from Me) ye can do nothing.—St. John xv. 5.

THESE beautiful, comforting, and also instructive words belong to that part of Christ's discourse spoken after the institution of the Lord's Supper, and while He was preparing Himself and His disciples for those unexpected and bitter events in the last day of His life in the Flesh. He spoke many other comforting words at the same time; commanded them to love one another; assured them of the hope of heaven; professed Himself the Way, the Truth, and the Life; promised them the Holy Ghost, the Comforter, and left them His peace; and then, to illustrate the relation between Himself and His disciples, He drew the simile of the vine and its branches.

Christ calls Himself the True Vine; the Father, the Husbandman; His disciples the branches.

He is the True Vine, because He is the source of all spiritual life and its fruits. He not only has eternal life in Himself, but He gives this life to all who by baptism are engrafted into Him and covenanted with Him; to all who are united with Him as the branch is with the vine, and so are parts of Himself and share His Life. In this sense, and for this reason,

He is both "the resurrection and the life;" not only giving us of His Life, but raising us up from death and the grave, because the life which He gives us is eternal.

The Father is the Husbandman. He is the originator and owner of the vineyard. The purpose of redeeming mankind through the Life-giving Vine originated with Him. The plan by which it was accomplished was devised by Him. His love cried out for man's salvation, and His wisdom produced the plan and carried it into effect. "God so loved the world," this sinful, guilty world, "that He gave His only begotten Son, that whosoever believeth in Him should not perish, but have everlasting life." "Behold what manner of love the Father hath bestowed upon us that we should be called the sons of God."

The branches of this Vine are the followers, or disciples of Christ. Here the simile is true as well of good and bad members, as of good and bad branches on the vine. The good in both cases grow and are nourished, and the bad are fit only to be cut off and burned. As in the vine we have good and bad branches, so in the Church we have good and bad members. These last are either sincerely deluded, or conscious hypocrites. They are not only useless in themselves, but an injury to the Vine. As such branches mar the beauty and hinder the growth of the vine, so such members are a scandal to Christ and His Church. As such members should be cast out of the Church, lopped off the Vine; so should also the evil tendencies of the Christian's nature be pruned that his graces may be more active and his fruits more abundant. So is character beautified and elevated also by affliction, loss of property, worldly disappointments and sickness; by which God shows us the nothingness of earth and the attractiveness of heaven.

But we are taught more of the necessity of abiding in, and communing with, Christ, than of pruning the Vine by excommunication. We are told, in words that are both a plea and a command: "Abide in Me, and I in you. As the branch cannot bear fruit of itself, except it abide in the vine; no more can ye, except ye abide in Me."

This shows the necessity of ingrafting into Him by baptism. For we are not members of Him by nature, and so cannot abide in Him unless we are, by grace and the Sacrament of Baptism, made a member. By nature we are depraved and utterly sinful; worthless as dead leaves or withered shoots; and we must be made alive and healthy, pure and holy, by incorporation by baptism into the Body of Christ, or into the True Vine. Then, by the exercise of faith and obedience, we will grow in grace and in the full vigor of spiritual life. For, as the branch receives from the parent vine its life, its strength, its mysterious tendency to exhibit exactly the same features and fruitage with the original vine, so the soul that is grafted into Christ, and abides in Christ and Christ in it, will have Christ formed in him, will grow Christ-like in thought and purpose and will and affections.

We cannot become this, we cannot bear spiritual fruit, except we abide in Him. This is a law of grace as of nature. It is impossible for a branch to grow or bear fruit, when severed from the source of its life. So no man can show any spiritual life apart from

Christ. But in Him, he begins to show the Christ-like disposition, he does the Christ-like deed, he grows into the Christ-likeness, he becomes more and more Christ-like in all things as he grows older in the faith and fellowship; until he has the full measure of the stature of the fulness of Christ.

Then, too, this union with Christ, as the branch with the vine, besides giving life and strength and causing spiritual growth, will be a new and blessed experience of Christ's love. He told His disciples that He had loved them even as the Father had loved Him. When we consider that the love of the Father for His Son was without variation, endless and infinite, sure as the existence of God Himself; and consider, too, that the Father loved us sinners with the same deep, infinite, endless love, so that He gave His own Son to live a life of humiliation and die the death of shame that we sinners might be delivered from our sins and be saved; then we can know also the wealth of love that is our inheritance, and know the grandest and noblest bond, not only between Father and Son, but between God and His faithful children.

Living in the communion of God's love, another result of abiding in Christ is that all true branches of the True Vine, all true members of the one Body of Christ, will love one another, not merely in obedience to Christ's command that they should, but because, as branches of the same Vine, they are bound by common affections, and sympathies, and purposes, to one Master, and hence must be bound by the same ties to one another. As Christ loved us and gave Himself for us,—a love that consecrated all His powers while living, and all His self-denials while dying, to the eternal good of those who were His bitter enemies, so should we love, not only Him but all who in Him are fellow-members and sharers with us of His gifts and blessings. His love is our model and the measure of our love.

Then, in all this abiding, faithful union and obedient following, in all this growth in grace and love, will appear the Father's glory—the pride and happiness of the Husbandman. As by its fruits we know the character of a branch, so by these we know, and the Father knows, that we and other members of Christ are true disciples, abounding in every good word and work.

As a last word let me ask: Is this true of us? Are we faithful and active members of Christ, branches of the True Vine, or is this only a theory in our lives? Do we bring forth the fruits of godly living, or are we withered and dead—fit only for pruning and burning? "By their fruits ye shall know them;" by *our* fruits we can know ourselves, of what sort we are. Let us look well into our hearts and pluck out from thence every evil growth, that we may be worthy branches in the vineyard of our Lord.

TWENTY-THIRD DAY OF LENT.

Jesus the Bread of Life.

I am the Bread of Life.—St. John vi. 48.

TO escape the multitude as well as Herod, and to seek quiet and opportunity for meditation, Christ and His disciples left Capernaum and went into a "desert place" east of the Sea of Galilee. But the multitudes followed Him in greater numbers now than usual, because pilgrims were on their way to keep the Passover who were attracted by the fame of His wisdom and His works—His Doctrines and His Miracles.

Towards evening the multitude became hungry, which Christ observed with tender anxiety. But there was nowhere to buy bread. The "desert" was uncultivated, barren, and uninhabited, and they were far from any help, and it was past sunset. There were among them all "five barley loaves and two small fishes," but what were they among so many?

Unwilling to send the multitude away, and yet unsupplied with food for Himself and disciples, Christ works the miracle of feeding the five thousand.

The next day, in the synagogue at Capernaum, and to much the same multitude, which still followed Him, with this miracle fresh in the minds of all, He made that startling announcement: "I am the Bread of Life"—"the living Bread which came down from heaven"—"not as your fathers did eat manna and are dead; he that eateth of this Bread shall live forever." "I am the Bread of Life." "The Bread which I will give is My Flesh, which I will give for the life of the world." And not only His Flesh, but also His Blood. "Verily, verily I say unto you, Except ye eat the Flesh of the Son of Man, and drink His Blood, ye have no life in you."

The people not only "strove among themselves, saying, How can this Man give us His Flesh to eat?" but "from that time many of His disciples went back, and walked no more with Him." Flesh to eat! Blood to drink! These are not only hard sayings, but contrary to the whole Law of Moses; and they forsook Christ. They thought only of carnal eating and drinking, and not of "feeding on Him in the heart by faith, with thanksgiving." It was like that other scene, in which Nicodemus wondered and questioned: "How can a man be born again when he is old?" But as there in baptismal birth the Spirit worketh in man's heart as the wind, which bloweth where it listeth, and we hear the sound thereof, but cannot tell whence it cometh or whither it goeth; so here, "blessed and sanctified by His Word and Holy Spirit," the eating is a spiritual, sacramental eating, and the Food is spiritual, sacramental Food. The mystery in Christ's words looks forward—one year—to the time when He should make, on Calvary, "by His one oblation of Himself once offered, a full, perfect, and sufficient sacrifice, oblation, and satisfaction, for the sins of the whole world;" and looks, also, to that "perpetual memory of His precious death and sacrifice, until His coming again," in the institution of which He took bread, saying, "This is

My Body," and took the cup, saying, "This is My Blood."

At all times there have been some who asked, with startled countenance or in incredulous tones: "How can this Man give us His Flesh to eat?" forgetful of what manner of Man He was, or what manner of Flesh He gives. We may ourselves have sometimes doubted or questioned, even in the least degree, but doubted, nevertheless; or, "have shrunk from the sacred Feast for unworthy reasons." That "Sacrament of piety, that sign of unity, that bond of charity,"* so designed by our Lord and Master, has often been a bone of contention. "How can He give us His Flesh to eat?" How can He, indeed? The Anglican branch of the Catholic Church has never undertaken to answer that question;—and wisely, for our Lord Himself has left it unanswered. How, it matters not; we need not know, and need not care. All that we do, and must, know is that Christ said of the one: "This is My Body," and of the other: "This is My Blood," and this we dare not doubt, and dare not question; nor dare we shrink from it and still hope to live the life that dieth not. How it is, is for God to know; that it is, is for us sufficient. The woman touched the hem of Christ's garment, and virtue flowed into her; she knew not how, and did not stay to question; but she believed, and touched, and was healed. Christ spake, and the Centurion's servant, who lay ill miles away, was healed in that self-same hour. He spake, and the blind saw, the deaf heard, the lame walked, and the dead arose. So

---

* St. Augustine.

He promised His Church that "the bread which we break is the Communion of the Body of Christ, and the cup of blessing which we bless is the Communion of the Blood of Christ;" and "He is faithful that promised."

In the Book of Proverbs the Lord says unto us all: "Come, eat of my bread, and drink of the wine which I have mingled." It is "the Bread of Life," life-giving and life-sustaining; and "he that eateth this Bread shall live forever." "Come, eat."

Yet, how shall we eat? In like manner as we receive and use all means of grace: by believing, and coming, and receiving. For, "he that cometh to Me shall never hunger, and he that believeth on Me shall never thirst." By coming whenever the Heavenly Feast is spread; by believing that it is Divine Food there offered; by believing that God's Word is true;— thus shall we eat. "He that believeth on Me hath everlasting life;" and, "he that eateth of this Bread shall live forever."

It is not a mere tasting, nor a bare subsisting. It is being fully nourished with the broken Body and shed Blood, with "all the benefits of His passion." It is to be filled with grace and life—with eternal life —with Christ's own Life. It is the highest and best eating; the life which it gives and nourishes is the highest and best life. Spirit communes with spirit, and Life with life. The Spirit here, verily, takes of the things of Christ and shows them unto us. We take, and partake, and are refreshed and satisfied. We come to meet our Lord, at our Lord's own Feast, and there He comes to meet us. We hear His words: "Eat, O friends; drink, yea, drink abundantly, O beloved." We come, we eat, we drink. Beneath the covering of what is visible to mortal eyes, the soul feeds upon the Son of God.

Yet, this is only a foretaste of a still better communion in the Church Triumphant. This is but the earnest of a still more glorious inheritance; the first-fruits of a more blessed harvest. If this that we now taste of the Bread of Life is so blessed, what must that be which, with saints and angels, we shall feast upon when the shadows and figures have passed away, and we behold, face to Face, the glory of the Word made Flesh, as He was in the beginning, and as He abideth forever!

But, alas! for the blindness and hardness of man's heart, how poor is oft-times our soul's appetite for this Heavenly Food; how little is our heart's desire for this Bread which angels eat; how little is our soul's craving for that Meat and Drink which giveth life everlasting? When our bodies hunger, we at once eat, or we grow impatient and distressed; if we lose one meal, we suffer; if we lose more, we grow weak; if we go a few days or a week without food, we get sick, and perhaps die. We make every effort to secure "the meat which perishes," but, "that Meat which endureth unto everlasting life, which the Son of Man giveth unto us" for the soul's health and happiness, oft-times remains for a long time untasted. The body must be fed; but the soul can do without its nourishment. The hunger of the body must be satisfied; but the craving of the soul goes unheeded. Yet, "man can not live by earthly bread alone;" but only when we "eat the Flesh of the Son of Man, and drink His Blood," have we any life at all. And "he that eateth My Flesh," said Christ, "and drinketh My Blood, dwelleth in Me and I in him," "and I will raise him up at the last day."

TWENTY-FOURTH DAY OF LENT.

The Church.

Head over all things to the Church, which is His Body.—Ephesians i. 22, 23.

WE have seen how Christ endeavors to teach us how intimately and organically He is related to His people, by the different aspects in which He makes us see Him in His Person and His Office. He says He is our great High Priest, showing thereby His Sacrificial Office and Atoning Work; and "the Good Shepherd," by which He tells us of a Fold into which He gathers His people, and of the tender care He takes over them; and "the Water of Life" and "the Bread of Life," by which He teaches us that He is our life-giving Nourishment and Refreshment; and "the True Vine" and we His branches, by which He shows us the living fellowship and communion He holds with us and we with Him, which also is shown in the figure of a building with all its parts fitly joined together growing unto a holy temple in the Lord, of which, He says, "I am the door"—and by the figure of a Body with its members growing in Him and deriving their life and vitality from Him. He speaks of the Church as a "Kingdom"—He Himself as the King—"the Kingdom of Heaven," and "the Kingdom of God;" nineteen of the thirty-two Parables teaching us facts and truths concerning it which can only apply to an earthly, visible, organized, ascertainable and self-perpetuating, life-giving and grace-bestowing Institution; an object of sight and knowledge as well as of faith. He thus sets the Church before us as a Fold, a Plant, a Building, a Body, a Kingdom, and Himself as our King, our Shepherd, our High Priest, our Head, our Life and Nourishment; the two together, Christ and the Church, forming, in their most vital bond, a concrete organism, an objective, generic economy.

The Church is a Divine Institution, not a voluntary "society;" with a Divine Commission and a human mission; coming from God and not from men; reaching out from above to gather men to God and to dispense to them the means of grace and the blessings of salvation, and not reaching up from below for the attainment of Christianity; "the kingdom of heaven" seeking men upon earth, and not a society on earth seeking the kingdom of heaven. "The kingdom of heaven is at hand," in "the Church of the Living God," and in the Church the life of Jesus Christ, her Head, is extended into the life of His members; and thus the Church, in her Corporate Life, is the extension of the Incarnation, an order of real objective existence of which He is the Head, of which the Holy Ghost is the Soul, in which the Apostolic Ministry are His "Ambassadors," and "stewards," who speak and act for Him and in His stead, and in which by the administration of the Holy Ghost through this Ministry the Life of Christ is given to all true disciples of our Lord, and nourished and increased in them until they reach the perfection of saints.

The Church is a Covenant, a continuation of the Old Covenant which God made with Abraham and crystallized in types and shadows, ceremonial and ritual, Fasts and Feasts, as well as of the promise God made to Eve in the Garden, of the Seed that should bruise the serpent's head. There has always been but "one Faith," as there has been but "one Lord, one God and Father of us all," made known in fuller and higher form, as man, by education in Divine things, was better prepared to receive higher revelations. There has been but one Covenant of God with man, and but one Church, though higher stages of its development, fuller revelations of its Divine truth; each stage and each revelation being, in man's aptitude for spiritual things and in God's manifestation of spiritual things, an advance on the preceding, until Christ Jesus completed, in Himself and in His work, a full and finished revelation of redemption. Linking Eden with the Patriarchal, the Theocratic, the Judaic and the Christian ages, the Church is no new thing, except that it is the realization and fulfilment of a promise that is nearly as old as our race; the old in principle and design, new only in the means by which the design is accomplished; the old trunk and branches, new only in fruit and foliage; the same Covenant as before, and as always, but a new Dispensation. Thus we are "fellow-citizens with the saints and of the household of God, and are built upon the foundation of the Apostles and Prophets, Jesus Himself being the chief corner-stone, as He was the central figure and objective point of revelation in every stage. He gave the Law, and fulfilled the Law; He made the prophesies and fulfilled them; He ordained the types and the whole ceremonial system, and they shadowed forth His own Atonement. He destroyed nothing, changed nothing. He continued the same Priesthood, the same typical sacrifices, the same moral law, the same Passover, the same Pentecost, though now all perfected by the addition of a new spiritual principle, even the very substance Himself who "filleth all in all."

The Church, thus, came from God, came to man; came with certain officers who are "stewards of the mysteries of God," and "ambassadors for Christ as though God did beseech you by us," praying all men "in Christ's stead" that they might be "reconciled to God;" came with pardon for sin and redemption from sin, and with manifold grace to enable men to lead a godly and righteous life ever after; came as the dispenser of pardon and grace, as the spouse of her Lord and the Body of Christ, bearing in her bosom the virtue of His Atonement, the fulness of His salvation, the Life which makes us fellow-members with Him and "sons of God;" came, therefore, as one visible, concrete Organism, with a Ministry of Divine origin, and rites and Sacraments of Divine institution, and a "form of sound words" that embodied "the Faith once delivered to the saints," by all of which she lays hold on men's minds and hearts, grafts them into Christ, endows them with His Life, nourishes that Life in us as her own, until we come to the eternal Kingdom. The Church, thus, is the Son of God articulated in Sacraments, explicated in symbols, organized into a visible body politic; His organized living and personal presence, exercising His functions as Mediator and Saviour; His earthly abode, as His natural body in Palestine formerly was; His organ through which He speaks to and acts upon men. Filled with Divine Life and Divine Power from Christ the Head and the Holy Ghost the Soul, this Body, the Church, is the living Christ Himself among us, administering to us the manifold grace of salvation.

Is any baptized, it is Christ Himself who, by the Holy Ghost, using His ambassador only as His instrument, puts forth His arm and grafts and incorporates that soul into His Body. Is any confirmed, it is Christ Himself who, by the Holy Ghost, using His Apostolic Minister whom we call Bishop as His instrument, stretches forth His Hand and strengthens and blesses with the seven-fold gifts of the Divine Spirit. Is any ordained, it is Christ Himself who, by the Holy Ghost, using His Apostolic Ministers as His organs, sets apart for the performance of sacred functions the man whom He Himself has called to His Holy Office. In the Holy Sacrament of His Body and Blood it is Christ Himself who sanctions and verifies every word that is spoken and every act that is performed, and who fills the Sacrament with Virtue for the spiritual and eternal good of His people, and by the hand of "the steward of the mysteries of God" administers it to His people. Has the Church set forth a Creed, or spoken authoritatively on any matter, it is Christ Himself who, by the Holy Ghost, speaks to us the unalterable truth through this His Mystical Body and Spiritual Organ. The Church, as Christ's Body and Organ, mediates Absolution to the sinner, and builds him up in faith and fellowship till he comes to "the measure of the stature of the fulness of Christ." The Church, as Christ's Body and Organ, is the one revealed way of salvation, bearing in her Bosom the grace and the blessings which are able to "save to the uttermost," and dispensing them to all those who will come into this way.

One word, now, about our relation to the Church. By baptism we and all Christian people were made members of this Mystical Body of Christ, and so we owe a duty to the Church as to Christ Himself. We owe her faith and obedience, devoted service and hearty support as to Christ Himself. Led by the spirit of Christ into all truth, the Church not only knows, but knows with certainty the Faith which is able to make us wise unto salvation; and not to hear and not to obey the Church, is therefore, not to hear and not to obey Christ Himself and the Holy Spirit. The sole object of going to church is not to hear sermons but to worship, and the highest form of worship is that which He Himself has appointed, that is, His blessed Sacrament; to stay at home is, therefore, to neglect or refuse to worship God, and to refuse to become a Communicant is to refuse to "remember" our Lord in the way He has commanded that we should.

To labor for the Church or the Sunday School in any capacity whatever, is laboring for Christ; and to neglect or decline to do such work is neglecting or declining to do Christ's work. To break from the Corporate Life of the Historic Church and go into schism is not only to rend the Body of Christ, but to break away from Christ Himself and become Anti-Christ. "He has not God for his Father who has not the Church for his Mother," says one of the Apostolic Fathers, since schism, as well as a church-less and creed-less life, is the logical outcome of unbelief and disobedience which God abhors.

You may have often heard well-meaning people

say, as I have, that it does not matter to which Church we belong, or whether we belong to any Church so long as we do what is right. They say this in the innocency of their hearts, but it is an innocency that is appalling. Why is it that the Apostles constantly warn us to beware of "false apostles," men "teaching for doctrines the commandments of men," men "carried away with every wind of doctrine," and "false teachers bringing in damnable heresies?" Why is it that we are warned against schism, and are taught to "keep the unity of the Body in the bond of peace;" and against heresy, and are told to "hold fast the form of sound words" and remain "steadfast in the faith once delivered to the saints;" and are warned against "anti-Christs" who have "departed from the faith?" Simply because Christ founded a Church and promised to be with that Church till the end of the world, against which the gates of hell should never prevail; and because this Church is what I have said she is—by lawful ministers and valid Sacraments, mediating God's grace and benediction. Does it not matter, then, whether we belong to this historic Church or to some human society—whether we belong to the Divine Body or to some man-made organization? Will God accept as equivalent our membership in one of the many human organizations? Does it not matter to Him who has Commissioned Apostles to break "the Bread of Life" till the end of the world, whether we receive it from such or not? Does it not matter to Him who said "Except a man be born again of water and the Spirit, he cannot enter into the kingdom of heaven," whether we are baptized or not? Does it not matter to Him who said "Except ye eat My Flesh and drink My Blood, ye have no life in you," whether we come to the Holy Supper or not? Does it not matter to Him or to us, what Church we belong to, or when and by whom founded, or what it teaches? It were a matter most strange if it made no difference—if God did not care. But the Scriptures and the early Christian writings show that it did matter very much in the early ages, and that necessarily it does matter, and matter very seriously, still.

My brethren, we have been brought by "one Baptism" into the "one Body" and are partakers of the "one Spirit." Let us thank God for the privilege, and endeavor to hold the "one Faith" as it has been attested and proved out of Scripture by God's Church from the beginning.

TWENTY-FIFTH DAY OF LENT.

HOLY BAPTISM.

As many of you as have been Baptised into Christ have put on Christ.—Galatians iii. 27.

WE do not wish to look at the Mode of Baptism in this lecture, especially as the *manner* of its administration is most trivial while the *matter* (the Formula and the Water) is the only and the all important consideration.

Nor do we wish to consider the subject of Baptism, as all well informed persons know that the proof is abundant and positive, from the writings of the Apostolic Fathers and the Decrees of Ancient Councils, that Infant Baptism has been the practice of the Universal Church from the beginning.

The *Effects* of Baptism are what we wish now to consider; neither *How*, nor *Who*, but *Why* we are, and must be, baptized, and what Baptism does in us and for us.

The Catechism, following the teaching of the Universal Church, says there are two Sacraments "generally necessary to salvation; that is to say, Baptism and the Supper of the Lord." At the time the Catechism was drawn up the word "generally" was used in the sense of "universally." The Church then, resting on Holy Scripture, teaches that there are two Sacraments "universally necessary to salvation." According to the Church's teaching, based on Christ's Word, Baptism is both a *necessary* Ordinance and a *saving* Ordinance; as Christ says, "Except any one," old or young, adult or infant, "except *any one* be born of water and the Spirit, he cannot enter into the Kingdom of God."

Whether "the Kingdom of God" here means the Church or Paradise is all one; for Baptism is the Door of Entrance to the one as to the other. By Baptism we are "made a member of Christ, the child of God, and an inheritor (heir) of the Kingdom of Heaven."

In Baptism a *character* is given us, an ineffaceable mark made on the soul by God, which distinguishes us not only from the "children of wrath" but from our former selves; so that once baptized we cannot be unbaptized and cannot be rebaptized, the character cannot be effaced and cannot be repeated.

This character consists in three Gifts: New-Birth or Regeneration, Remission of Sins, and Endowment with all the Spiritual Helps to Grace.

Baptism is the Sacrament of Regeneration—"the washing (or laver) of regeneration and renewing of the Holy Ghost." As by our natural birth we are brought into the natural world and into the family of "the first Adam," so we are by our regeneration brought into the spiritual world and into the family of "the Second Adam." As we derive our natural being and life from the first Adam, so we derive our supernatural being and life from the Second Adam. The old man is buried and the new man is raised up in us. This is done in Baptism, which is a new-birth into a new state, a translation from the kingdom of evil to the kingdom of grace, from the world to the Church or Kingdom of God. Every Divine grace and every blessing of the Gospel is promised only "in Christ;" and by Baptism we "put on Christ," are grafted into Him, annexed to Him, incorporated into Him, clothed upon by Him. By Baptism, "Christ is formed within us," and is born within us as really as He was born of the Virgin Mary. Baptism is Christ's Sacrament of Self-Incarnation. By its power and operation we become "partakers of the Divine Nature," that is, the Incarnation of Christ is extended to each one of us individually, as it is to the Church generically, through the re-creation of our whole nature in Him and the infusion of His Divine Life into us. "By one Spirit we are all baptized into one Body" — "baptized into Christ," into the Church which is the Body of Christ—the Corporate Life of Christ on earth. So that it is due to our Baptism alone that we can say, "Christ liveth in me." By Baptism we are, as members of Christ and participators in His very Self, adopted into God's family (which is again the Church), reconciled to Him, brought into grace and favor with Him. He becomes our Father and we become His children in a new and higher sense than before, our Father through Christ our Elder Brother, and through the Church (His Body) our Spiritual Mother. By the spirit of adoption," given us in Baptism we call God "Our Father." And thus, mystically one with Christ, and of "the household of faith" or the family of God, we are "heirs of the kingdom of heaven"—of that part which is here on earth with all its grace and blessing, its absolution and benediction, and of that which is hid from human eyes in the Paradise above.

Union with Christ by Baptismal regeneration—the only way by which we are made one with Him—brings us two gifts. One of these is Remission of Sins. We "receive remission of sins by spiritual regeneration," says the Prayer Book. In the Creed we profess "one Baptism for the remission of sins;" so that Baptism is there declared to be the Sacrament of Absolution. In the New Testament it is everywhere spoken of as such. St. Peter, preaching to the assembled people on the Day of Pentecost, said: "Repent, and be baptized every one of you for the remission of sins, and ye shall receive the gift of the Holy Ghost." Ananias said to the converted Paul at Damascus, after his eyes were opened: "Arise and be baptized, and wash away thy sins." Our Lord God, speaking by the mouth of His prophet Ezekiel, said: "I will pour upon you clean water, and ye shall be cleansed from all your filthiness." The Apostle Paul likewise said to the Corinthians, "ye are washed, ye are sanctified." All sins are "washed away," "remitted," forgiven—those previous to Baptism by the baptismal act itself, and those since Baptism by the eternal character of that act, or by the union with Christ into which we have been brought, and the atmosphere of forgiveness in which we live and move "in Christ." So that, though worthily deserving to be punished for our sins, we are at all times within the reach of forgiveness, and are readily forgiven if penitent and believing.

The second gift or consequence of our Baptismal Regeneration in Christ is the endowment with all

Spiritual Helps to Grace that are in the Church. This comes with the eternal character of our union with Christ. Being, in her Corporate Life, the Body of Christ, and being made members of that Body by Baptismal Regeneration or ingrafting, we have not only every grace given us by which the new life within us is developed and sustained, but we are taken up into such close, living union with Christ, that we are one with Him as He is one with the Father; and this is fulness of grace and blessing to them that by faith and obedience will profit thereby. "Because we *are* sons, God sends forth the spirit of His Son into our hearts, crying Abba, Father." By Baptism we became sons, and this sonship endowed us with the Holy Spirit, as with every gift and blessing the Father can bestow upon sons. We may destroy the new life of the soul, as we may "quench the spirit" or deny the Faith; but we are members of Christ and "sons of God" still—dead members and prodigal sons; and we are part of that spiritual Family still, and have a claim to all that is conveyed to man from God by whatsoever channel it is brought. God gives Himself really and fully through Baptismal birth, but He may not be received wholly by any, and may not be received at all by many, as they may or may not appropriate the gifts by faith. Yet He is there and is given; it is a Divine act complete in itself, which we make real to us by a perfect faith, a perfect obedience, and a perfect life. So that if we are faithful in our discipleship all the means of grace in the Church will, by regular use, build us up a spiritual house in the Lord until we come to the perfection of saints in the Triumphant Kingdom.

This is precisely what was wrought by Circumcision in the Old Dispensation, which has given way to Baptism in the New. On account of this identity of purpose St. Paul calls Baptism "circumcision made without hands," spiritual circumcision, that is, circumcision by "water and the Spirit." As that was God's covenanting act to man, by which He became their God and they became His people, so is this. As by that the child was taken into the Theocratic Kingdom, so in this he is planted into the soil of the Church. As in that he was heir of all covenanted blessings, civil and ecclesiastical, temporal and eternal, so in this the blessings of Christ's Incarnation, Redemption, Resurrection and Ascension are made his own, and are ever with him, even when his faith is weakest or his life unworthy, as a firm and sure foundation upon which he may confidently fall back for pardon and peace. In the darkest hours, in the strongest temptations, in the fiercest assaults of Satan, God's unfailing mercy vouchsafed in Baptism, His Covenant Vows, Christ's abiding presence, the indwelling Holy Spirit, are as strong and "everlasting arms" beneath and around us, if our faith will but look up and behold. "Heaven and earth shall pass away," but God's promises, Christ's word, confirmed to us by an everlasting oath and sealed to us in Baptism, shall never fail; and shall be as an anchor of the soul both sure and steadfast, all through life, and in death, and beyond, leading us from grace to grace here, and there from glory to glory.

TWENTY-SIXTH DAY OF LENT.

Examination and Eating.

Let a man examine himself, and so let him eat of that Bread and drink of that Cup.—I. Corinthians xi, 28.

FALSE doctrines, improper ceremonies, and strife had crept into the Corinthian Church in connection with the Holy Eucharist. So far did they carry their division and contention, that St. Paul was obliged to administer his Apostolic rebuke and say, "Now this I command you."

It is painful to think—painful to every true Christian as it must have been painful to Christ Himself—this sharp controversy was about the Sacrament of Unity and Love. The Apostle therefore teaches them its character and its meaning, its Divine Institution and its blessed fruits; how to prepare for it, and how to partake of it. Among other things he commands self-examination as a sweet preparation for receiving the Holy Supper, lest "eating and drinking unworthily, we eat and drink damnation to ourselves, not discerning the Lord's Body." There must then be a high and awful Mystery in the Sacrament; and if so, what is it?

Instituted by our Lord, and filled with the fulness of His grace—the quickening virtue of His own Life—it is the Lord's Supper. It is no common meal, as, after Consecration, it is no common bread or ordinary wine. By Consecration the Elements become

Sacred. They become the Lord's Vehicles by which He imparts to us the living virtue of His Body and Blood.

In one sense the Sacrament is a Memorial of our Lord's Death, as His Apostle says, "ye do show forth the Lord's Death till He come." Breaking the Bread, we call to mind the broken Body of Christ; pouring the wine, we call to mind the shed Blood of Christ. It is a Memorial of that Sacrifice of Christ which was made necessary by our sins, yet which secures for us remission of sins and life everlasting.

But it is more than a Memorial. It is a Feast; a Feast, not on bread and wine but on the Body and Blood of Christ. In the Sacrament Christ gives Himself to His people as the true bread from heaven, possessing the seal of everlasting life. The body takes the natural elements of bread and wine; but the soul, in mysterious communion with its Lord and Saviour, feeds upon Christ's Body and Blood. Christ dwells in the soul, and the soul in Christ. "My Flesh is Meat indeed, and My Blood is Drink indeed. He that eateth My Flesh and drinketh My Blood, dwelleth in Me and I in him." That Holy Supper is therefore no empty form or ceremony, no symbol of an absent Saviour; but is mysteriously filled with living substance, that substance being the Body and Blood of the very Christ Himself.

It is, therefore, the Sacrament of Union and Communion with Christ. By mystery divine He is the Vine, and we are branches of Him; He is the Head, and we are His members; He is the living Temple, and we are living stones built up into a spiritual house in Him. There is perfect union and communion between the vine and its branches, and a head and its members, or a building and its parts; so there is also between Christ and His people, who are "flesh of His flesh and bone of His bone." We feast on the hidden manna, and He shows us the secrets of His Heart's Love, and the mysteries of His Kingdom. In it He reveals Himself to us as He does not unto the world; and having our eyes opened as were those at Emmaus, we see Him in the breaking of His Bread, we feed upon Him, and live.

Thus it is to our entire being the Sacrament of nourishment and refreshment. In Holy Baptism the evil that we have by nature is washed away; in the Holy Feast the good that we have not by nature is given us. Mysteriously do we eat of the Bread of Life and are filled. Mysteriously do we drink of the hidden Fountain of grace and are refreshed. We receive newness of life, and our "life is hid with Christ in God." We receive fulness of blessings in "the Cup of blessing which we bless." We receive life—Divine Life—ever more and more abundantly as we come more and more to His Feast; life that dieth not, life that knows no ending, life that even now partakes of immortality because it is "risen in the likeness of Christ's resurrection," and is "hid with Christ in God." In ourselves we are dead, yea, we die daily; but, behold! in Christ we live, we live evermore; for, "he that hath the Son hath life." The Sacrament of the Lord's Supper is the Vehicle of Life, the Son's own Life. Here we see Him face to Face. Here we touch and handle things unseen, and grasp with firmer hand eternal grace. And this is bliss, yea, this the Gate of Heaven.

"Let a man examine himself, and so let him eat of that Bread, and drink of that Cup." No wonder the Apostles left this warning and this command. Holy Mystery! it is to us either a savor of life unto life or a savor of death unto death. But with what thoroughness and by what standard shall we examine ourselves? For it is possible that we may search too severely, and condemn ourselves when mercy tempereth justice; or too slightly, and so dishonor the Feast by lacking the wedding-garment. By what standard, then, shall we examine ourselves?

The Church, like a tender and loving Mother, puts her invitation to the Holy Sacrament in most comforting words: "Ye who do truly and earnestly repent you of your sins, and are in love and charity with your neighbors, and intend to lead a new life, following the commandments of God, and walking from henceforth in His holy ways, draw near with faith, and take this holy Sacrament to your comfort, and make your humble confession to Almighty God." Repentance, confession, faith, love and charity towards our neighbors, obedience to God's Law,—these cover all that is necessary to partake worthily of our Lord's Blessed Sacrament. Simple, indeed, is the requirement, for the true Christian is always in that frame of mind which is acceptable to God, and which realizes the Gospel as a living fact, and so is penitent, believing, loving and obedient. And to him the Sacrament is not only a blessing full of grace and nourishment, but it works that transformation of body and soul by which he is more and more translated from the earthly into the heavenly, and from earth to heaven.

TWENTY-SEVENTH DAY OF LENT.

In Remembrance of Me.

Do this, in remembrance of Me.—I. Corinthians xi. 24.

AS the end of Christ's Ministry drew near, He realized more fully the separation that would follow between Himself and His disciples. He should be parted from those He had gathered around Him, He to return to His Throne, and they to go out into an unbelieving and persecuting world, and suffer stripes and imprisonments and death for His sake. That little company of disciples, so attached to their Master, so linked to one another by many hallowed ties, should now be broken, and scattered into all parts of the earth. Those pleasant and secluded spots, made so memorable and sacred by Christ's astonishing miracles, wonderful discourses, and fervent prayers, should be given up, left behind, and thought of only as haunts of the past. Torn from Christ, they should be left, apparently, without a leader, without a teacher, and without a defender and friend. They should be exposed to the merciless attacks of Scribes, and Pharisees, and doctors, priests, and Levites, and people. The whip-cords, the dungeon, and the cross, with all that indescribable suffering which these objects meant, should darken the lives of this faithful band. All these things, and much more, occurred to Christ as He thought of the near approach of His betrayal and Death. Sad was His countenance, sorrowful His Soul.

But Christ gave them promises, and what were they? "When the Comforter is come, whom I will send unto you from the Father, even the Spirit of Truth, which proceedeth from the Father, He shall testify of Me, and shall teach you all things, and bring all things to your remembrance, whatsoever I have said unto you." But more than this. He promised to be with them Himself. Giving them the Great Commission to preach the Gospel and disciple all nations, He said: "Lo I am with you alway even unto the end of the world." Yet more than this still has He promised. He Himself will not only be *with* them but *in* them; in them both by the indwelling of Himself and His Holy Spirit, and by a Mystical Presence for which He was then about to provide. He Instituted the Sacrament of His Body and Blood that it might be fulfilled as He said: "He that eateth My Flesh, and drinketh My Blood, dwelleth in Me, and I in him." Such promises as these amended for the loss they should sustain in His personal separation. Really and truly in them, meant closer fellowship with Him than they ever held before. They would gladly suffer persecutions, if He should be in them and they in Him. What were all the pleasures and joys of life, compared with so great joy in such blessed inter-communion as that! With them and in them; what better thing could they want, or what more could He promise!

Jesus, the same night in which He was betrayed, took bread and the cup, blessed each, gave to the Apostles, with the request to partake of them, and to do this, in future, in remembrance of Him; for this should be the sign and the seal of that blessed fellowship and indwelling.

The Holy Communion is the Sacrament of Remembrance. It is a memorial of His Death, "for as often as we eat this Bread, and drink this Cup, we do show the Lord's Death till He come." But a memorial not of His Death only, but of His Life. In it His whole Being, His whole Self, with all that He did and taught, every feature of His Mission that enters into the Atonement, is presented before our eyes and to our faith.

Beholding with our eyes the natural elements of bread and wine, we behold by faith and spiritual sight the Body and Blood of our Lord Christ. Receiving with the mouth the natural elements of bread and wine, we receive by faith and sacramental eating the Body and Blood of Jesus Christ our Saviour. How we do, we cannot tell; that it is a fact, we know and believe. But not any single act or fact, isolated from the rest of Christ's Life, is brought to remembrance. Death was but the culmination of His Mission, but the issue of His Redeeming Work, since "without shedding of blood there is no remission." The entire Life of Christ in all its phases and features was Messianic and Mediatorial; and every distinct part, no less than His Death, is brought to remembrance. We remember His humiliation and Incarnation, His Circumcision and Infancy—nursed, watched, carried about on His mother's arms, and borne into Egypt; as sitting in the Temple, at the age of twelve, being Confirmed by the Doctors in His Covenant rights and eating His first Paschal Supper; we remember His Baptism, Fasting, and Temptation; His walks up and down Palestine as the Servant of man, not ashamed to eat bread with publicans and sinners, not ashamed to mingle with the poor, the lowly, the contrite, and the outcast, going about doing good with His love unceasingly active in behalf of all, not being ministered unto but ministering with an unsparing Hand and an unfailing devotion.

We remember Him on that awful night of sorrow with the Apostles in the upper chamber, they watching His every movement, listening to every word, divining His very thoughts, and He Instituting the Sacrament of His Body and Blood. We remember His agony and Blood Sweat, the Deliverer Himself on bended knees in lonely Gethsemane, a suppliant before the Father, and Himself crying for deliverance. We remember Him a prisoner, led by armed soldiers, surrounded by an angry mob,—then a condemned criminal led forth for execution. We remember His Cross and Passion, exposed to the gaze of all His revilers, His life-blood escaping from Him drop by drop for their eternal salvation. We remember His Death and Burial, Resurrection and Ascension, on earth the first-fruits of the dead, and in heaven the first-fruits of Redemption. We remember Him as our only Intercessor and Advocate before the Father, pleading His Perpetual Sacrifice for us and for our salvation.

But we dare not stop here. As a Memorial, the Sacrament not only pictures to us the whole of Christ's Life and Work, but puts us in mind why He lived and why He Died. He lived, and suffered, and died, and rose not for Himself alone; not because it pleased Him to do so; not for an exhibition of power; not to arouse wonder and astonishment. But for your sins and mine, for your salvation and mine, for you, and me, He became Incarnate, and labored, and was Crucified, gaining by His Sacrifice eternal victory over sin, Satan, and death, and atoning for our sins before a merciful Father.

"In remembrance of Me." O, how inclined we are to forget Him! In the busy stir of our lives we think much of what we are doing for ourselves, and little of the work Christ has done for us. We need this Sacramental remembrance, not alone for our spiritual nourishment and growth in grace, but for our faith that we may make His Passion more real to us; we need it for our hope, that we may be assured that by it are life and immortality more and more brought to light; we need it for our love, that love may abound yet more and more for Him who loved us even unto death; we need it for our penitence, that by the great suffering which our sins have caused Him we may see the greatness of our sins; we need it for our tenderness, that by the sorrows and sufferings which it brings to remembrance our hard hearts may be softened and melt away in tears; we need it for our thankfulness, that we may see and know and feel the price which our blessings have cost Him, and the blessings which that price has purchased.

> "According to Thy gracious word,
>   In deep humility,
> This will I do, my gracious Lord,
>   I will remember Thee.

> "Remember Thee, and all Thy pains,
> And all Thy love to me;
> Yes, while a breath, a pulse remains,
> Will I remember Thee."

But it is no mental but a Sacramental remembrance. We are to do it oft, and as oft as we do it remember Him. O, the glorious Gift which the Sacrament conveys, and the precious consolation that it brings and leaves with us for our heart's health and our soul's peace!

TWENTY-EIGHTH DAY OF LENT.

In the Upper Chamber.

It is the Sacrifice of the Lord's Passover.—Exodus xii. 27.

IT was Thursday in Holy Week. Christ and His disciples left the home of Martha and Mary, in Bethany, towards evening, and, by the path so familiar to them over the Mount of Olives, came to the Holy City to keep the Passover. In the morning He had sent two of His disciples in advance to prepare "the Upper Chamber" in what is supposed to have been St. Mark's house.

It was their last walk from Bethany to the City until after His Death; and they walked it in stillness and mysterious dread, foreboding a coming storm. They come to the house, enter it, and sit down at the table to partake of what they did not then realize—their last Paschal Supper; not, however, without some strife and contention—perhaps as to who should have the chief seats—so that He, who had come from God and should go to God, in the bitterness of a sorrow which human heart never felt before nor since, had to teach them the lesson of humility and administer a tender rebuke by washing the disciples' feet. But most fitting was it for the Master to wash His disciples, for, as He stooped and washed their feet, so He should stoop to the lowest depth of humiliation and wash His people from their sins.

This act revealed to the disciples the mystery of the Incarnation.

Look at the meaning of the Passover, whose feast they had come to celebrate. Instituted on the night of their deliverance from Egyptian bondage, when the first-born of the land was slain, it was ordained to be observed ever after as a perpetual commemoration of that event. The offering was to be a lamb "without spot or blemish or any such thing." The victim was to be slain as an offering for sin, and its blood sprinkled on the door-posts as a sign to the Avenging Angel, who should then pass over the house thus protected. The sacrifice was also to be eaten, for it was to be incorporated, in the most intimate, living way, with the life of the worshipper. It was to be eaten with unleavened bread — the "bread of affliction" — to remind them of their Egyptian servitude. It, however, besides looking back to that deliverance from bondage, looked forward, also, to a spiritual deliverance; and each celebration of the Passover involved a prophetic reference to the coming of that Great Salvation. It was a grand type of an Offering for sin that was to be made "when the fulness of time was come." It was the shadow of a Substance that was to be given in the future. They ate of it in faith that they were then partakers of a communion with God, which He would, in His own good time, bring to perfect realization. They sacrificed in faith that it would, in God's mysterious way, atone for their sins, and give them His covenanted grace. But it was still a type and a shadow only of good things to come. The fulfilment should be made in the Offering of the true Lamb of God—the Messiah.

Here, at the table in this Upper Chamber, oh, Wonder of all wonders! was the Lamb Himself, celebrating the Passover which was a type of His own sacrifice, eating the spotless lamb which was a type of His sinless Self. He whom the Paschal Lamb prefigured and anticipated, was here, the fulness of time having come; and He was commemorating the prophetic representation of His own Death. But only so as to bring to an end the Old Testament Dispensation, which crystalized itself around the Passover; to fulfil and abolish its types and shadows; and to institute, instead, a new, better, and higher Sacrament—the Memorial of His broken Body and spilled Blood. As with a sacrament He began His ministry, so with a second sacrament He ended it. "For in the night in which 'Christ our Passover' was betrayed, He took bread, and when He had given thanks, He brake it, and said, Take, eat, this is My Body, which is broken for you: this do in remembrance of Me. After the same manner also He took the cup, when He had supped, saying, This cup is the new testament in My Blood: this do ye, as oft as ye drink it, in remembrance of Me. For as oft as ye eat this bread, and drink this cup, ye do show the Lord's Death till He come."

Here, at the table in this Upper Chamber, was the true "Lamb of God that taketh away the sins of the world," Priest and Victim, superceding one feast by another of far deeper and diviner significance, as it was of diviner Food. Here He was, at once the Host and the Food, the Pascha and the Dispenser of it, the Slayer and the Slain, offering up Himself, in the Feast of the Old Dispensation and in the Sacrament of the New, a Sacrifice for the sins of His people. "Without shedding of Blood there is no remission." Here, then, oh mystery of all mysteries!—in the Blood of the Paschal Lamb He was already offering His own Blood; in the wine of the New Sacrament He was already spilling that precious Life which ended its suffering on the Cross. The elements in His Hand—emblems of His broken Body and shed Blood—were already, in effect, a "showing forth of the Lord's Death," and pictured to His sorrowing Soul the agony and bloody sweat, the scourge and the thorns, the nails and the spear, in His sacred Head, and Hands, and Feet, and Side. What must His thoughts, His emotions, yea, His sufferings, have been, as He ate the lamb, and as He broke the bread and poured the wine, knowing that they represented His Cross and Passion!

As the Paschal Lamb had to be eaten to be of any avail to the worshipper, thereby bringing himself and his offering into living union and communion; so we must eat this bread and drink this cup if we would have life in us. "Except ye eat the Flesh of the Son of Man, and drink His Blood, ye have no life in you." It is only when we receive these into our soul that the Sacrament finds its completion, and the blessing of the Sacrament—"eternal life"—is given.

When we do come to eat this spiritual Food, how do we come into His holy Presence? How do we behold those earnest looks of inquiring Love? How do we see the melting tenderness of His Countenance? How do we look into those Eyes of His, beaming with unfathomable love, and hear those words of consolation such as never man spake? The scene in the Upper Chamber was "the Lord's Passover," and the Lord Himself was keeping it; and yet, alas! the hand of treachery was even there with Him on the table. Is it ever so now? The false heart of one of His disciples was eating "the sop" from His own Hand, and yet, alas! filled with the basest ingratitude, and leprous with the foulest sin. Is it ever so now? What are our feelings and conduct when we "keep the Feast?" What they would have been had we been in that Upper Chamber on that wonderful night, such they should be now. Can we say, "Lord, it is good for us to be here?" or, if Christ spoke to us, would He say to us, "Thou gavest Me no kiss?" Can we say, as the Mystic Bride spoke to the heavenly Bridegroom, "I sat down under His shadow with great delight, and His fruit was sweet to my taste. He brought me to the banqueting-house, and His banner over me was love?" Oh, these cold, dull, faithless, unloving, ungrateful hearts! These deaf ears! These blind eyes! We come to meet our Lord at "the Lord's Passover," and He comes to meet us; but we have no realization of His Presence, and no depth of love in our hearts. "We are prone, in the noise and busy stir of the present, to forget the Oblation of our Lord on the Cross in the far-away past. Amid our daily doings we are prone to forget what He has done. In our many blessings we forget how the curse rested upon Him. In our many happy hours, we forget His sorrows. Sitting refreshed in the shadow, we forget the Tree of Life that shades us. Warmed by His Love, we think not of the Sun of Righteousness from whence those beams come.

Drinking at the stream, we forget the Fountain whence all refreshing waters flow."* Eating "the Bread of Life," we are ungratefully forgetful of Him who feeds us, and of Him who is the Food.

"It is the Sacrifice of the Lord's Passover," and the Lord Himself is here, and the Lord Himself is offered. What does this mean to us? Is it food and nourishment to us; or is it empty of any blessing? Is it the seal and pledge of His Presence and the promise of the bright day of His second advent; or is it a meaningless ceremony? "Whoso would live, hath where to live, hath whereof to live; let him come, let him believe, let him be incorporated, that he may be quickened."†

---

* Henry Harbough.
† St. Augustine.

TWENTY-NINTH DAY OF LENT.

GETHSEMANE.

And they came to a place which was named Gethsemane; and He saith to His disciples, sit ye here, while I shall pray.—St. Mark xiv. 32.

THEY have kept the Feast of the Passover in "the Upper Chamber"—the Saviour and "the twelve." Many significant words were spoken, and many wonderful things were done there; but these had to come to an end. "When they had sung a hymn" they went forth into the silent night, and to the Mount of Olives—the Saviour and now "the eleven." One had gone to another part of the city and upon another mission.

'Twas the last watch of the night, yet from houses here and there they could still see light shining. The Passover Moon was at its full, and the Orient's brow was set with the Morning Star. A deep silence subdued them as they passed along the narrow, winding streets, and out of the Eastern or St. Stephen's Gate, near the walls of the Temple, down the steep slope of the ravine and across the Kidron which was pushing its black and angry waters along a hundred feet below; and up the green slope beyond—the eleven, with mysterious dread and awe, behind, the Saviour, with bowed head and sorrowing heart, in front. With dull footsteps they pass in and out of the shadows.

Perhaps at the Kidron the solemn hush of the silence is first broken, by that last warning of all, of the Old Testament prophecy that this night the Shepherd should be smitten and the sheep scattered. Staggered by this prediction He turns to St. Peter with the individual prediction that Satan would that night sift him as wheat is sifted, but that He had prayed the Father that his faith fail not. Protestations and vows are multiplied in answer to these predictions. They will never forsake Him. St. Peter, though he should die with Him, yet he would not deny Him. Ah! little did they know of the mighty wonders of that night—of the terrible things that night should bring forth.

They now come to the entrance to Gethsemane, and they enter. They know the place well. Often had they come into its enclosure and sat beneath its shady grove of olives, in the cool breeze which came from the mountain above. Inside the gate, or perhaps in the keeper's house or in the oil-press, He leaves eight of the eleven—the three more favored ones, who had also been with Him on the Mount of Transfiguration, who stood nearest to Him and loved Him best, He takes with Him farther in. Even these He soon leaves while He goes forward a little, falls down on His face yonder, and prays that this cup, if it were possible, might be taken from Him. He has entered "into the Valley of the Shadow of Death." In the dark shadows of the trees, the "powers of darkness" are making a fierce onslaught upon His Soul. The violent winds of hell are sweeping over His prostrate form. He groans in the spirit. He wrestles in prayer. A cold flood of anguish—of terrible agony—breaks over Him. He is "amazed" as He looks into the horrors which treachery was even then preparing for Him. He is "sorrowful even unto death." Hear that cry of awful grief and suffering that comes from His Soul again and again, as Satan's anger lashes itself into fury against His shrinking Body: "Father, if it be possible"—if it be possible, Oh, Father—"let this cup"—this awful cup of most horrible sorrows—"pass from Me." That cup was the fear, the dread of death—death accompanied by overwhelmingly brutal shame. But surely not that alone. There was mingled in the dregs of that cup whose bitterness so shook His Soul to its very centre, all the burden of the sins of the whole race of mankind, in its apostasy and fall, in all their most wonderful and mighty accumulation. This—the sense of sin and of death as "the wages of sin," was it that filled the cup to its brim, and which He drank to the bottom.

To fallen man, who has the taste of death always in his soul, death is not so terrible; but to the Christ, the Unfallen Man, the cup of bitterness which He emptied, not for Himself, but for sinful, guilty, brutal humanity, was filled with deepest humiliation and utmost divine wrath, as well as bodily torture and mental anguish. The shaft of death was buried deep into His heart, for man's sake and by man's own hand; and that shaft was poisoned by the world's sin. We cannot tell, as He, the depth of that sorrow. We cannot know, as He, the depth of that suffering. We cannot taste, as He, the bitterness of that hour. Now kneeling, now prostrate; fallen under the weight of man's guilt, "offering up prayers and supplications, with strong crying and tears unto Him that was able to save Him from death," the Soul of our Saviour was in its last and fatal agony. He who had often before put demons to flight, was now prostrate on the ground in tears. He whose voice calmed the winds and the sea, and called spirits from their graves, was now trembling, with the broken accents of supplication and prayer on His pale lips. He who for three years did such mighty wonders in all the land, whose fame spread abroad into all countries, was now recoiling from the possibilities of that hour. Yet He is resigned. "Father, not My will but Thine be done."

Again and again He prayed. In the loneliness of His Soul, in the heaviness of His heart, in the desolation and gloom which His sufferings cast over Him, He came to His three most favored disciples, not once but twice, for that sympathy and help which He then so much needed and craved. Alas! in the heaviness of their hearts, in the weariness of that hour, in the grief of their souls, they had fallen into deep slumber, unappreciative of His terrible suffering. What a grief this must have been to His heart! As with many of us, He found them not watching, but sleeping. "He looked for some to have pity on Him, but there was no man, neither found He any to comfort Him." "He must tread the wine-press alone."

But that kneeling and prostration, those groans and prayers, that agony of Body and Soul, are not all that we see or hear in the gloom of that hour. The "crown of thorns" had not yet been forced down upon His pale and death-like face; the sharp nails and spear had not yet pierced His flesh; yet on His brow, on His garments, and on the ground beneath

Him were the signs of a "Bloody Sweat"—great drops of blood. Oh! what must His inner torture have been—the torture of His Soul, to force from His sacred Body that "bloody sweat!" What unutterable agony, what unfathomable grief that must have been, that could release itself only in this most remarkable, most awful way! Here, too, might He have said: "Behold and see if there be any sorrow like unto My sorrow."

Thus the Saviour spent that hour in the shadows of Gethsemane. But the end came at last, and with it came victory. Treachery had done its work. He saw the lights of His pursuers in the distance; yet a light "whose fountain is the mystery of God," shone upon His Soul, voices stole out of the chambers of the vaulted sky, and a form knelt beside Him like unto the form of God, and nerved Him with holy strength. He collects His disciples for the meeting. His Soul, awhile ago in great grief and excitement, is now calm; and in "meekness, whose divinity is more than power and glory," He says: "Rise up, let us go; lo! he that betrayeth Me is at hand; the Son of Man is betrayed into the hands of His enemies."

Oh, beloved! Should Gethsemane, with its awful but hallowed story, not be dear to us all? Should it not find a well of love deep down in our hearts, for the victory that agonized struggle gained for us? In our struggles, our anguish, we can go to Gethsemane, and, as well as human heart can, live over the terrible struggle and fearful horrors of that hour of our Saviour's Passion, and from it get an inspiration and a blessing.

"When heart is weary,
  When eyes are teary,
  Or life's way dreary,
I seek the shades of Gethsemane.
  And thither straying,
  Believing, praying,
  I hear Christ saying,
    'Oh! Trust in Me.'
  Then with confession,
  And intercession,
  And new profession,
  Hopeful I press on,
    Oh, Christ, to Thee!
  And feel Thy love more
  Sweetly than e'er before
  Stealing my heart o'er,
In the lone shades of Gethsemane.

"Charmed on this sacred ground,
  As dies each worldly sound
  In the deep peace around,
  Sweeter than rest is
    This spot to me.
  At thy foot, Olivet,
  Fondly I linger yet;
  Think of His bloody sweat
    And agony!
  Whilst with confession,
  And intercession,
  And new profession,
  Hopeful I press on,
    Oh, Christ, to Thee!
  Saviour, Thy love more
  Sweetly than e'er before,
  Steals all my heart o'er
In the sweet shades of Gethsemane."

THIRTIETH DAY OF LENT.

Watching with Christ.

Watch ye therefore, for ye know not when the Master of the house cometh.—St. Mark xiii. 35.

What, could not ye watch with Me one hour?—St. Matthew xxvi. 40.

WE combine these two passages, the one a command and the other an exclamation of surprise, as showing not only the weakness of three of Christ's disciples—the three of "the Twelve" who were nearest to Him in affection—under the most trying circumstances and the most awful moments of Christ's earthly life; but as showing our own plain duty in response to Christ's wish, and the weakness and unwillingness of our nature to obey in this as in all Christian duties that oppose the natural tendency of our hearts.

The Master bade the three watch with Him one hour while He goes yonder to pray; but instead of watching they sleep, though happily for them it is the sleep of sorrow. The Master suffers; they sleep. Such is the coldness and weakness of human hearts. For this has not only been once, and in the last sad scene of our Lord's earthly life; but it has often, has always been the case. While our Lord watches we sleep. While He suffers we give no heed. While He is in agony we are at ease. While He endures tortures we have pleasure.

Let us question ourselves more closely. Let us imagine our Lord in our midst, as indeed He is. Look upon Him and hear Him say: "Tarry ye here, and watch with Me." What is our inclination, our desire, our impulse? Hear Him say: "What, could not ye watch with Me one hour?" What can our answer be? Would it not in almost every instance be, "No, Lord, I cannot"?

And why? Is it for want of grace to help? Certainly not. Is it for any unwillingness? Perhaps so. To watch with Christ requires little of the head, but much of the heart, little mental effort but much loving affection. We can do almost anything else but this, and we can do anything else much better. We can read a novel all day and all night; we can pass a whole night in dancing, the whole previous day in preparing for it, and the whole next day in sleeping off the effects; we can do wearisome or difficult labor without complaint; we can spend hours at the concert or theater with unflagging attention, it matters not what the state of the weather; we can spend an hour or more in any occupation of business or pleasure without weariness; but to watch with Christ one hour, to spend one hour in prayer, or meditation, or worship, at Lenten services or other services—"No, Lord, I cannot—at least not often." We think the demand presumptuous; the mere thought of such a thing is full of heaviness and puts us to spiritual sleep. The three who first heard this exclamation of surprise, were excused with the words, "the spirit, indeed, is willing but the flesh is weak;" but this cannot be said of us. Our flesh is indeed also utterly weak, but our spirit is unutterably unwilling. We have no fervency of spirit, no earnestness of faith, no true devotion of heart. Our hearts are cold, our faith is dead, our devotions are weary, our affections are earthbound. In short, we do not love God enough, and love ourselves far too much. We think not enough of God, and all too little of our relations to Him here and hereafter. We hide ourselves behind other people, and are fond of losing ourselves in a crowd. We delight to say, "we have erred and strayed," but all notion of "I have erred and strayed" is foreign to our thoughts. We are fond of saying, "we have offended against Thy holy laws;" and in saying it we have, perhaps, some other's sins, great or small, in mind; but we think not of ourselves and say, "I have offended against Thy holy laws." We do not like to look upon ourselves singly and alone, which, however, one day we must when, in the nakedness of our hearts, we shall stand before the piercing Eye of God. And so we do not watch as we ought; we do not pray, we do not serve, we do not obey, we do not worship with that willingness and devotion, that fervency and zeal, which the Master requires of those who profess to be of His Household.

But let us ask, what is it to be not watching—to be spiritually sleeping? We may be wakeful enough as to the things of this world, but unmindful and indifferent as to the next. We may be keenly active in this world's affairs, but wilfully ignorant and careless as to the things of the next. We may be all eyes and ears in all that concerns our worldly success, but blind and deaf and dumb in all that concerns the soul's eternal happiness. We are sleeping, not the sleep of sorrow, but the mad and fearful and dangerous and deadly sleep of wilful sin. Sin has dominion over our souls; sins of habit dwell in our hearts, sins of character deform our being; and woe be unto us, if the Master of the house come now, come suddenly, and find you, or me, in this state! Yea, He is here, standing in our midst, looking into our hearts, seeing our spiritual sleep in the toils of sin, though He has bidden us to watch, and has given us grace to watch with Him. What answer shall we give? Can it be that we cannot, will not watch; that we cannot, will not shake off these sins; that we will not break these fetters that hold us to evil habits and wicked deeds? Shall we say: "No, Lord, I cannot"?

But to be spiritually asleep one need not be in wilful sin. We may be of good speech and conduct, of pure habits and excellent character, regular in our attedance at Church, and, perhaps, in our attendance at the Lord's Dear Feast, respected and loved by all, and still be asleep. How? Simply because there is too much worldliness in our hearts, and not enough heart in our religion; because our affairs of this life are of primary importance to us, the affairs of the next only secondary. We may be earnest in spiritual things, but more earnest in worldly. We may take interest in our soul's salvation, but greater interest in the "piece of ground which we must needs go and see," or the "five yoke of oxen which we must needs go and prove," or the wife we have married. So that while we have interest and earnestness in a measure, we still have not enough to be wholly out of sleep and watchful as we ought to be.

Who can tell when the Master of the house cometh

—at even, or at midnight, or at the cock-crowing or in the morning? He delayeth His coming, and that hour knoweth no man, nor the Son, but the Father. But when He does come, at death as at the Great Day of His Advent, it is a fearful thing to be found sleeping, a fearful thing to have lamps without oil, a fearful thing to be left by the Heavenly Bridegroom in that darkness and gloom into which we ourselves have gone.

Again, let us question ourselves—let us look into our hearts, at our spiritual state; let us ask, were the Master of the house to come now, would we be satisfied with what He should find, satisfied with that state, satisfied with ourselves, with our feeble devotions, with our listless, heartless prayers, with our half-hearted service, our cold-hearted praise, our wandering thoughts, our dryness of spirit, our weariness and sleepiness? Could we be satisfied?

If not—and I dare say none of us could be—then we must do as He bids, watch with Him, not only one hour, but always, and until our eyes shut to all things sinful and our hearts are filled with all the fulness of the Divine in the world that is to come.

We must watch ourselves, lest we lag, or loiter by the wayside, sporting with earth's flowers on the brink of Eternity. We must set a watch over our lips, guard our ways, and make constant search of our hearts, without a thought of trouble or weariness, plucking up all bitter weeds in the heart, mellowing the soil by prayer, and nourishing "the fruits of the Spirit" with the dew of heaven.

And we must watch for Christ, and watch with Him; watch for His coming as if He were already here; watch for His appearing as if we were already with Him. "We know not when the Master of the house cometh." "Watch ye, therefore." "Blessed are those servants whom the Lord, when He cometh, shall find watching." But what if, instead of these words of blessing, we shall hear the exclamation of surprise, "What, could not *ye* watch with Me one hour!" and the added words of sorrow and grief, because of our worldliness and sinfulness, "I know you not!" "He cometh as a thief in the night," and "behold! He cometh quickly." "The Lord direct your hearts into the love of God, and into the patient waiting for Christ," so that it may be well with you at His appearing.

THIRTY-FIRST DAY OF LENT.

BETRAYING CHRIST.

Verily I say unto you, that one of you shall betray Me . . . The Son of Man is betrayed into the hands of sinners.—S. Matthew, xxvi. 21, 45.

IN the Upper Chamber, and during the Paschal Feast, our Lord was looking into a dark abyss that was yawning at His very Feet, and seeing the terrible storms of anguish that would that night sweep over them all. With pitying Soul He saw the last and fatal step of one of His Twelve; and He longed to save by appealing, with a sop, to all that was human, all that was tender, all that was merciful and good in the heart of Judas. He saw too, how, in those terrible hours, one should deny Him, and be almost torn away from his Master; how all should be scattered to the four quarters.

With a lonely, sad, troubled, suffering soul; with sorrow and anguish growing heavier and pressing more bitterly into His Heart; with thick darkness not only hanging over Him, but gathering within His Being, He said, "Verily I say unto you that one of you shall betray Me." Behold that Face as He utters this; behold grief and love, human pain and divine majesty blending in His Features. Behold it as He looks out upon this group of wondering, horror stricken men—now upon John, then upon Peter, then upon James, then upon the others one by one, and lastly upon Judas. See the tear of mortal woe, the shuddering of His Frame, as His Eye rests upon this last one and He says: "one of you shall betray Me." What a fearful announcement to make to such a devoted band! What perfidy! What treachery! One of these His own most intimate companions, who had received His favors, who had shared His secrets, who had been admitted to His friendship; who were called to such glorious work, to such high honors; who were to receive such vast powers, and such precious gifts; who, under the Spirit's guidance, were to be the founders of His Church, the foundation stones of that Divine Building, the princes of that spiritual kingdom sitting on twelve thrones; one of these who now sat with Him at table, ate with Him the Paschal Lamb,—one of these should betray Him. David had long before said of this one: "Yea, Mine own familiar friend, in whom I had trusted, which did eat of My bread, hath lifted up his heel against Me." In mingled love and sadness, Christ makes known to the Twelve that this prophecy of David is about to be fulfilled, and fulfilled by one of their own number. One of you, "he whose hand is with Me on the table," "he that dippeth with Me in the dish," "he to whom I will give the sop," "he it is that shall betray Me."

We wonder not that they all became exceeding sorrowful and anxious; that each of the Eleven, in conscious innocence of any thought of betraying—conscious only of intense love for their Master, yet with countenance o'er-spread with death-like paleness and fear, asked of Him, "Is it I? Lord, is it I?"

A few hours later, we see a band coming up towards Gethsemane, of armed soldiers, and led by one of the Twelve.

Let us imagine our Lord in our midst. Suppose Him here before us, gazing upon us with tender, loving Eye, yet with a Heart breaking with sorrow. Hear Him again saying those words which so startled the little group of Apostles sitting with Him at the table. Hear Him addressing us with a voice trembling with emotion, yet filled with pity: "Verily, I say unto you that one of you shall betray Me." The words would astonish us, and call forth strong denials. Betray our Lord! Sell Him for paltry silver or gold, and our birthright for a mess of pottage! Give Him the hypocrite's kiss! Deliver Him to His enemies to do Him harm! Be the willing means of torture! Put Him to shame, to death! Have the mockery of heathen soldiers, the insults of a furious mob, the smiting and scourging, and, last of all, the crucifixion of an innocent, a sacred Being, blamed upon me, and have such crimes laid at my feet! We deny and protest. But we hear a sweet, quiet voice say: "Even so, My son; one of you which eateth with Me shall betray Me." Not a stranger, not a known enemy, not one who was openly hostile, not one of those who had long plotted against Him and lain in wait to kill Him. From such a one it were easy to bear insult and harm. But not one of these. One of His "own familiar friends" should do this wrong; one who was intimately associated with Him, who had received His favor and His love, one that eateth with Him—such a one should be traitor.

We begin to fear and tremble. Have not we eaten

with Him? Have not we knelt at His table? Have not we received His Food? Have not we received His favors, His friendship, His love? Have not we called Him our Lord and Master, followed Him for, lo! these many years, been part of His Household, members of His Family, partakers of His blessings? Can it be that He is saying this of us? Can it be that we are traitors to our Lord? And so we, too, begin to ask that little, but very important, question, "Lord, is it I?" Am I a traitor to Thy cause? Have I sold Thee to Thine enemies? "Is it I?"

Why not you? Why not I? Have we lived such pure lives that we are above suspicion? Is our conscience so clear that we find no lingering shadow of a former sin? Is our character so stainless that our bitterest enemies, with all their blackest arts, cannot even taint it? Remember even a St. Peter denied Him, and came near betraying Him; why may not we? Remember, also, that each of the twelve in fear asked; "Lord, is it I?" And if one of them, why not one of us?

Yet, however horrible, however fearful a thing it is, we do betray our Lord, and some of us, alas! too frequently. One may be regular in his Church attendance, an occasional communicant; yet in his daily life he may bring forth no fruits of godliness; perhaps unkind or unforgiving in disposition; perhaps hard, covetous, or dishonest in business; perhaps unchaste, passionate, or blasphemous in language; perhaps self-indulgent, or intemperate in habits; in short, he may be a Sunday saint but a week-day sinner. Such a one is simply a hypocrite; and the kiss of the betrayer was the crown of hypocrisy. One who has God's name on his lips, now in praise and then in blasphemy; one who comes to the Sacrament with Satan in his heart; one who bends his knee one moment to God and the next to Mammon, comes very near the traitor's kiss. Were such a one ever moved by conscience to ask: "Lord, is it I?" he would hear, if he listened for it, the same conscience give the quiet, reproving answer: "Thou hast said."

Or again. One may be blameless in life, consistent in conduct, pure in speech, God-fearing and God-loving; yet at heart too cowardly to confess Christ before men. He hears words of evil and pretends not to be shocked. He listens to blasphemous language and sits idly by. He hears the saints ridiculed, Christian duties laughed at, Christian principles assailed and dragged into the dust; and he speaks not a word in defence. He is a hypocrite of a different sort. He pretends not to be moved, not to be shocked; and if he were to ask the question, "Lord, is it I?" "he would certainly receive the answer, "Thou hast said." His cowardly conduct, fearing the world too much to reprove it of wickedness, is selling his Lord into the hands of His enemies.

So there are many other hypocrisies, many other ways of betraying the Master, many other cases that bear a fearfully strong likeness to the kiss of the Traitor. And they are not so very rare, either. We need not go out into the streets, nor into the lowest dens, to find them. Too often have we, even we, betrayed Him. Too often have we, by our indolence, our neglect, our lukewarmness, our indifference, our faithlessness, our selfishness, our worldliness, our hypocrisy, our cowardice, our covetousness, our unkindness, our passion, our evil words, sold Him to His enemies, delivered Him to the mob to be mocked and insulted, delivered Him to the Cross. Too often have we sent a pang of sorrow into His Heart by our inconsistency. The sins of Christians are the griefs of Christ; and we are of that number who grieve Him by numberless shortcomings and misdeeds, of greater or lesser degree, but all betrayals of our Lord.

THIRTY-SECOND DAY OF LENT.

The Denial.

He began to curse and to swear, saying, I know not this man of whom ye speak.—S. Mark xiv. 71.

WHAT must have been, to our Lord, one of the saddest incidents in Holy Week, was the denial by St. Peter, one of His chief Apostles, one of His most trusted friends. He was the first to confess Christ, and yet the first to deny Him; and deny Him soon after he had eaten with Him the Holy Supper—Sacrament of Unity and Bond of Fellowship.

Let us recall the story; and as we do so let us ask if it has not repeated itself often in our own lives.

On the way to Olivet and to Gethsemane our Lord told His Apostles that "all should be offended because of Him that night;" and that the "Shepherd should be smitten and the sheep scattered." Peter, as if stung by this want of confidence in his attachment to our Lord, said: "Although all shall be offended, yet will not I." Our Lord looked into St. Peter's heart and saw what St. Peter yet knew not of. "Verily," said He, "this day, even this night, before the cock crow twice, thou shalt deny Me thrice." But St. Peter "spake the more vehemently, If I should die with Thee, I will not deny Thee in any wise. Likewise also said they all." Deny Thee, Lord! Deny Thee, whom I have confessed to be "the Christ, the Son of the living God!" Whom I have so devotedly followed for three happy years! Who has been my daily comfort, my hourly delight! Whom I have served with willing hand and loving heart! Behold, I "have forsaken all and followed Thee." Deny my Master and my Saviour!—Even so.

Our Lord predicted the incident; St. Peter protested. Look now at the scene in the High Priest's palace. A maid approached and, seeing St. Peter warming himself, said: "Thou also wast with Him." Peter denied, saying: "I know not, neither understand I what thou sayest." And the cock crew. Our Lord, with that Eye which saw the denial long hours before, saw it now realized. What a shudder it must have given His frame, now weak with fasting and weeping! What a bitter pang it must have given His Heart, already torn with that sharp suffering and agony in the Garden! Oh, what can the heart of man not bring forth! Even the heart of His "most familiar friend!"

But another maid saw him again, and began to say to them that stood by: "This is one of them," and he denied it again. That Eye was still upon him. Again that frame quivered; again that pale face moved with agony; again the shaft pierced His Soul.

But a little while after they that stood by said again to Peter: "Surely, thou art one of them." But he began to curse and to swear, saying: "I know not this man of whom ye speak." And immediately while he yet spake, the cock crew. And the Lord turned and looked upon Peter. Significant was that look, reproachful and eloquent in the extreme; and St. Peter understood it quite well, for he "remembered the words of the Lord, and went out and wept bitterly."

Our Lord's persecuting enemies, thirsting for His blood, could have poured into His cup of anguish no deadlier bitterness than these bold denials with cold, naked, perjured oaths to God and imprecations on himself. All the scourging, buffeting and spitting; all the mocking, cursing and insult by His enemies were as nothing compared with one of these denials by His disciple; and yet, instead of one there were three, and the last with oaths and curses. The anguish of the condemnation, the humiliation and the shame, none of these, perhaps, burnt into His Heart so much as these denials by the chief of the Apostles. Of all the twelve, our Lord relied upon him to strengthen his brethren; and our Lord prayed that his faith fail not. Yet here, not long after that prayer was uttered; not long after St. Peter's vehement professions of devotion, his faith not only failed, but he denied that faith; and had not our Lord told these twelve, told St. Peter at a most solemn time: "Whosoever shall deny Me before men, him will I also deny before My Father which is in Heaven." Oh, the bitterness of that thought!

Have you taken any of this to yourself? Have you seen yourself in St. Peter's conduct? Have any recollections of past weakness come to your mind as we looked at St. Peter's denials? and have you said, "Thus, also, have I done?"

Not thrice, but daily and hourly, have we denied our Lord—you and I—in one way or another, in thought, word, and deed. By "blindness of heart, pride, vain-glory, and hypocrisy;" by "envy, hatred, and malice, and all uncharitableness;" through "inordinate and sinful affections, and the deceits of the world, the flesh, and the devil;" by "false doctrine, heresy, and schism;" by "hardness of heart and contempt of God's Word and commandment;" by other "evil and mischief" do we Christians frequently or constantly deny Christ, whom yet we profess to love and to serve. You and I hear the voice of the Baptist on the banks of the Jordan and in the wilderness, calling to repentance, for the Kingdom of Heaven is at hand; but we are not attracted by the sound. You and I rush out with the multitude, with "Hosannas" on our lips; and the next day we cry "Crucify Him! crucify Him!" We join with Christ's followers when He is riding in triumph; but thin the ranks when the cross is to be meekly borne. Our voices are heard loud in professions when professions cost us nothing; but when theory is to be reduced to practice, we are offended at Him, and scatter. When He most needs disciples to confess Him before men, His professed friends and followers melt away. Many follow His star when it promises blessing; few follow Him to the Mount bearing His reproach. You and I have shamefully denied Him, and often.

But let us look again at St. Peter. He denied and fled. Out into the night he fled; but not into a night of gloom, and remorse, and despair, as that other false Apostle. There were stars in that night; and so did stars of hope and promise shine into St. Peter's soul,—the brightest of all stars that Christ had prayed for him. He wept hot tears, but not of despair; tears of sorrow and penitence; and the Angel of Repentance led him back, heart-broken but steadfast in faith, to the feet of his suffering Lord.

So with us, and with all for whom Christ died.

Even in our greatest sins Christ intercedes for us, and prays that we may forsake our sins and live. When we have fallen, when we have denied Him, when we have fled from Him, let us think of St. Peter, and mingle our tears, confessions, and humiliations with our prayers and Christian hope. Let us pray that the angel of grace fail us not, but may keep us steadfast and fervent unto the end of our life and into the very gates of death.

THIRTY-THIRD DAY OF LENT.

The Mockery.

And when they had platted a crown of thorns, they put it upon His head, and a reed in His right hand: and they bowed the knee before Him, and mocked Him, saying, Hail, King of the Jews! And they spit upon Him, and took the reed, and smote Him on the head.—St. Matthew xxvii. 29, 30.

CAN we ever fully realize what all this was to our Lord? Let us to-day go back to that sad, sorrowful, shameful scene. Three times was He mocked. Once in the High Priest's palace, in the presence of Caiaphas and the Sanhedrin; and mocked by His own people. "They spit in His Face and buffeted Him, and others smote Him with the palms of their hands." These people for whom He had done so many acts of kindness; to whom He had given so many blessings; to whom He had spoken so many words of encouragement; whom He taught, and loved, and healed, and pardoned; over whom He wept and for whom He prayed; His own covenant people mocked, insulted, and maltreated Him.

Caiaphas sends Him to Pilate, and there again is He mocked; not by His own people but now by "the soldiers of the governor," the heathen hirelings of a heathen ruler. They "put on Him a scarlet robe;" they crown Him with "a crown of thorns;" they gave Him a reed "as His sceptre of royalty; "they bow the knee before Him; and they, too, "spit" and "smite."

Pilate sends Him to King Herod, and again, a third time, is He cruelly insulted. He "with his men of war set Him at naught, and mocked Him, and arrayed Him in a gorgeous robe, and sent Him again to Pilate." One such brutal assault was not enough, nor two; but, like the three temptations in the wilderness, and like the three denials by St. Peter, and like the trials before three different courts, He was mocked and maltreated three distinct times, before three different high officials, by three different bands of people. And these three times may not have been all, nor may the recorded means of torture have been all; for St. Luke says that "many other things blasphemously spake they against Him," and we may suppose many other things also did they unto Him.

See how they ill-treat Him. See them lay hands on Him, and rudely pull and push and jostle against Him. See them uplift their clenched fists, and deal heavy blows upon His sore and weary Head and Body, and utter blasphemous words. See the servants smite and buffet Him with the palms of their hands, and the soldiers scourge Him with a reed, and with the biting lashes of a whip, the blows falling not on His Back only, nor on His Limbs, but on His Head and Face, as He stands with His Hands tied firmly to a pillar, a foul handkerchief blind-folding His Eyes, until His Blood trickles and flows. See them strip Him of His garments and put a scarlet robe upon Him; plat a crown of thorns for His Head; put a reed into His Hand for a sceptre; bow the knee before Him, and hail Him King, mocking His claims; and, most shameful and insulting of all, see them spit upon His sacred Person, and into His meek and holy Face—the Face which saints and angels have long time adored in ceaseless contemplation and wonder. Oh, to what depth of brutality and shame may man not descend! Into what low acts of violence, into what degrading conduct, may man not fall! What vulgar speech may he not utter! What shocking deeds may he not do! How debased may he not become in his soul, how depraved in the desire of his heart! To what repulsive conduct may he not stoop! Highest of all created beings, but a little lower than the angels, and made in the image and likeness of his Creator, and yet lowest and meanest, and vilest in conduct and speech!

And who is He whom they thus maltreat, and mock, and insult? What has He done to merit their indignation and scorn? Passing strange—yea, passing all understanding and wonder—He who is so rudely handled and so shamefully insulted is the "Maker and Upholder of all things visible and invisible;" Son of Man, yet Son of God; the Lord of heaven and of earth, of men and of angels; their own Lord God, and ours. He certainly "made Himself of no reputation" when He "was made in the likeness of men." He certainly "humbled Himself" to the lowest plane of human life when He came among such as these. Having at His beck and call legions of angels to do His will, yet the prisoner of a hostile power, and the meek, uncomplaining, unresisting victim of an angry, dissolute, insolent, and vulgar mob. Lord of the living and the dead, whose power is omnipotent, yet passive under the harsh usage of servants and soldiers. He whose Tongue uttered naught but love and blessing, and yet was "sharper than a two-edged sword," here was silent and speechless; "as a sheep before her shearers is dumb, so He opened not His Mouth." He whose Eye was overflowing with kindness and sympathy, and yet could strike terror into the hearts of Pharisees, yet suffered Himself to be blindfolded by lawless and wicked hands. He who created and dwelt in eternal Light, and who for awhile covered Himself with that Light on the Mount of Transfiguration, yet here suffered Himself to be covered with the soiled garments of a low, brutish, mocking soldier. He whose Countenance was soft as the moonlight, and whose Face beamed with infinite love, turned not that Countenance from the sight of such shame, "nor hid that Face from spitting." Buffeted and smitten, "the plowers plowed upon His Back and made long their furrows." Bruised and beaten, He had indeed "no form nor comeliness, no beauty that we should desire Him." "His visage was so marred more than any man, and His form more than the sons of men."

It is indeed a sad, a shameful, a disgraceful scene. Behold your Lord and your God "give His back to the smiters, and His cheeks to them that pluck out the hair." Behold Him dishonored and despised, trampled under foot of man, dragged in the dust, and "set at naught," as though He were the earth's curse or the filth of society.

Yet it was so ordained, and so were the Scriptures fulfilled. Little did the mocking crowd think that all these things had a divine meaning. Little did they know that the scarlet robe was the most fitting garment for Him who is King of kings and Lord of lords; or that the crown of thorns symbolized that diadem which He had laid aside for awhile when He became man, and which He would take up again when His life of shame and suffering, of which this was an important part, was over; or that the reed in His hand told of the sceptre of His Kingdom, which is a righteous sceptre, and of His Throne which is forever and ever; and bowing and saluting, they did not think that not only they but all men must adore Him, and that "every knee shall bow, of things in heaven and things on earth, and things under the earth, and every tongue confess that He is Lord." Unwittingly, unknowingly, unconsciously did they bear witness to the Truth; and in the lowest and meanest part of their mockery these mockers were prophets.

But let us leave this amazing scene and come to ourselves. We have heard our Lord once say: "Take My yoke upon you, and learn of Me, for I am meek and lowly of heart." We also heard Him say: "Ye shall drink indeed of My cup." Answer your heart, then, how do *you* behave when the cup of bitterness is offered you; when you are smitten and afflicted, wronged and insulted; when you are made to endure not the hundredth part of that which your Lord was made to endure for you? How do you take it? Even when unintentionally wronged or misunderstood we smart and resent it; and much less is the spirit of meekness and lowliness in our hearts when we are wilfully mocked and insulted.

But this is not all. Not only is the exceeding beauty

of God's grace of humility not in us, but we often help the scoffing crowd to mock and debase our Lord. Witness much of your conduct and mine. Call to mind many of your words and deeds, and mine. They belie all our Christian professions, and put our Lord to an open shame. He blesses us, and we wrong Him. He gives us His grace, and we smite Him with our curses. We follow the crowd from the High Priest's palace to the Governor's Hall; mingle with the servants, and take part with the soldiers; return His kindly look with an angy scowl, and call aloud for His daily crucifixion.

Oh, that our hearts were humbled; that the meek and lowly spirit of our Lord were in us; that we were like unto Him at all times, in all things, but especially when persecuted, as He was, for righteousness' sake.

THIRTY-FOURTH DAY OF LENT.

Behold the Man.

Pilate saith unto them, Behold the Man.—St. John xix. 5.

WHAT means all this commotion in Pilate's Judgment Hall so early in the morning? Why this vast assembly of people—Scribes, Pharisees, Priests and common people, with eager yet angry faces and excited movements, mad with passion and religious hatred? What do they here? Surely no part of the Paschal Feast is to be kept in such a place; and a Roman governor is not necessary to a proper observance of all that is prescribed.

No. And this is perhaps the first time that the Paschal Feast was ever interrupted by such scenes and incidents, this the first coarse mob that ever unhallowed the holy season.

Though, whatever else they do, they will not enter the Hall. That would be too shocking and defiling during this holy Feast. They must not, dare not, enter a heathen tribunal now. They must not defile themselves by contact with anything that is unsanctified. To accuse falsely, to procure false witnesses, to clamor for innocent blood, to induce a world-fearing Roman governor and politician to pronounce an iniquitous sentence, all this was no defilement—no sin; but to go into Pilate's Hall they dared not. So they stand outside and shout, and surge, and clamor, and curse.

The crowd near the entrance falls back, and a still greater clamor goes up from the hoarse throats of the multitude. We see Pilate within, surrounded by his soldiers, and just behind him the form of One whom we have seen before. But how changed is His appearance! His face is deathly pale. "A crown of thorns" is on His head, its long, sharp prongs tearing His holy brow. "A purple robe" is about Him, put there by scornful soldiers to do Him mocking homage. They have buffeted, bruised and smitten Him with the palms of their wicked hands, and with a reed. They have "scourged Him" with the terrible lash. They have spit upon His mangled frame and into His bleeding face. Blood from the piercing thorns is flowing down His face and upon the purple robe. He is weak and shivering with pain and suffering; emaciated, worn out, insulted, weary.

Pilate looks toward the crowd and, pointing to Him, says: "Behold the Man!" What Man? The prophet answers: "A man of sorrows and acquainted with grief;" "He was despised and rejected of men." See His patient weakness; see the tender, holy love in His Eye; see that longing look as if beseeching for an answering love and sympathy. Can He indeed be One who "perverteth the people?" Can He have done anything deserving of condemnation or death? "Behold the Man," as Pilate points Him out to us.

Is this He who "went about doing good;" who ministered to the needs and wants of all who called upon His Name; who wept over the sins of His people; who was never more like Himself, and like God, than when hearing and answering the prayers of sorrowful hearts; who was "touched with the feeling of our infirmities" and came with healing in His wings? Was it for this that He made the blind to see, the deaf to hear, the dumb to speak, the lame to walk; that He healed the sick, cleansed the leper, and raised the dead? Was it for this that He taught, and wept, and prayed?—Even so.

For did we not once, a few years before, hear another say: "Behold the Lamb of God which taketh away the sin of the world?" Behold Him now, "brought as a lamb to the slaughter," "stricken, smitten of God, and afflicted;" and behold in Him, O, wondrous love! your Saviour and your God. As He looks out upon this maddened mob yelling for His blood, hear Him say: "Is it nothing to you, all ye that pass by: behold, and see if there be any sorrow like unto My sorrow." No, never any like His, and His was the sorrow of God.

It is enough to melt any heart; and Pilate brought Him here, hoping at sight of His poor, weak, tortured, bleeding, almost dying condition, wholly innocent as He was, they would "repent them of the evil" and show sympathy and pity. But no. What flinty, stony hearts must theirs be! For love they give Him hatred. He showed them kindness; they despise Him. He went about doing good; they return evil for good, and wish Him harm. Seeing Him only adds to their passion, and Pilate's appeal only awakes a fiercer clamor. From their howling throats, from their icy hearts, comes the cry, "Away with Him," "crucify Him, crucify Him;" "His blood be on us and on our children."

See the tear on His cheek as He hears these terrible words. See the trembling of His lips, the shuddering of His limbs, the heaving of His bosom, the death-like pallor on His face. Hear that heavy, sorrowful sigh. He looks out over the city of His father David—the city of His Father God—towards the Temple of the Most High, which lifts its magnificent walls high over Mount Moriah, and points its pinnacles to heaven as if invoking Divine aid or warning the people of God's wrath upon the evil-doer. He looks out over the people who are so dear to His heart, and yet so sinful and wicked. He thinks of His happy childhood days when He learned the prophecies at His Mother's knee, and of the work the Father had given Him to do, now that He was a man, in fulfilling the prophecies and bringing salvation to this city and this people. He thinks of the words He had said but a few days before, as, standing on Mount Olivet, He looked over this same city and this same people: Oh, blessed city of My fathers, type of that which is above, "as an eagle stirreth up her nest, fluttereth over her young, spreadeth abroad her wings," so would I have "kept thee as the apple of My Eye, and hid thee under the shadow of My wings;" "thou that killest the prophets and stonest them which are sent unto thee, how often would I have gathered thy children together, even as a hen gathers her chickens under her wings, and ye would not." Buffeted, bruised, smitten, scourged, mocked, insulted, degraded, blasphemed, despised, rejected—was it for this that He was sent; was it for this that He came; is this the Father's will; is this fulfilling the prophecies; is this salvation? "Behold the Man," and see and consider if there be any salvation in Him.

We are not the only ones who see as Pilate cries: "Behold." He also sees. As we see Him, He sees us, you and me, face to face and eye to eye. Blind-folded, yet out of the depth of His bleeding heart He sees. He looks to us for help. He appeals to us for sympathy. He pleads for our love. Past the power of saving Himself, yet even now, even yet He longs to saves us. But our hearts, too, are cold and stony. We are in sympathy with the mob. We are playing our part in the awful act. Our sins are laid upon His back. We crowd our iniquities into His very Soul. We wound His heart with our transgressions. We, too, have brought Him to this; and we are among the loudest who shout, among the noisiest who clamor for His Crucifixion. Oh, think of your past life, and then think of Him. Lay bare the sins and follies of your heart, and then "behold the Man" in shame and derision, "an offering for sin," that you and I may not die the death of a sinner, but live in Him.

Oh, bitterest of all suffering! Most wonderful of all love! that sorrows and languishes for our sins, and inherits the woe which we alone do merit! There was no spot in our hearts by sin untainted; yet He washed us clean within with that precious Blood which now runs down His bruised face and beaten back, which stains His purple garment and the tessellated floor beneath His feet. King of our hearts, let us ever bow the knee before Him. As our Saviour and our God, let us ever "Behold the Man," and find in Him rest for our weary souls.

THIRTY-FIFTH DAY OF LENT.

CARRYING THE CROSS.

He, bearing His Cross, went forth into a place called the place of a skull.—St. John xix. 17.

If any man will come after Me, let him deny himself, and take up his cross daily, and follow Me.—St. Luke ix. 23.

LET us take our thoughts back to the last morning of our Lord's life on earth. During the few short hours before the dawn of that day memorable events transpired. He had kept the Paschal Feast, and had Instituted the Sacrament of His Body and Blood. He had watched and prayed in Gethsemane, where, alone, in desolation and despair, agonized in mortal conflict with sin, the deep waters of sin rolled up to His Soul. He had been betrayed, hurried on to Annas, to Caiaphas, to Pilate, to Herod, and again to Pilate; from indignity to indignity, from torture to torture, until we see Him now, in the midst of a dense throng of soldiers, and men, women, and children, from the Temple, the shops, the bazaars, the markets, and the streets. The clamor, "Let Him be crucified," had conquered the deeper feelings of Pilate; and, unrefreshed by food or sleep, His pallid Face bearing the blood-marks of the crown of thorns, His Back showing the long furrows of the lash, He was led to the Crucifixion "as a lamb led to the slaughter," bearing, according to custom, the weight of His own Cross.

Can we, who are surfeited with ease and comfort, realize the shamefulness of the Cross, or the deep humiliation of bearing it? Everlasting Son, God Incarnate, Lord and Giver of Life, Creator of all things—even of these men whose infuriated hatred cried out against Him and who hurried Him to His Death; He staggered under the weight of a Cross that was to bear His lacerated and bleeding Form. He, who came to the very lowest level of human life to redeem it, refused not this last and bitterest humiliation. The procession moves out of the gate. With Him are two malefactors, also bearing each his cross. The people scoff and shout; the soldiers urge them on; the women weep. But that Cross with the weight of human sin is more than He can bear, notwithstanding the Divine strength underlying His Human weakness. His Frame trembles, falters, faints. And yet He who so often put forth His Divine power in helping others will not help Himself; He who so often put forth His Hand in behalf of others, is silent and passive in His own extremity. Who will lift Him to His Feet? Who will help Him with His Cross?—No one. There is none in all that multitude that will have pity on Him; they only mock and shout all the more. And as for His disciples, they have all fled; and He truly treads the wine-press alone.

You say, perhaps, if you had been there *you* would have lifted the prostrate Form; you would have assumed, or at least shared, the heavy burden; you would have braved the scoffing mob, and given the strength of your body with the devotion of your heart to the poor and weary Man.

But you forget. The cross was a thing of scorn and reproach, of shame and disgrace; and instead of coming to the Sufferer's aid, we, more likely, would have been among those who scoffed. It was a loathed instrument of execution, and not the emblem of salvation that it now is; and you and I would not have carried it then, for we do not carry the cross that is given us now.

We all have our crosses; and we must bear them daily, bear them willingly and cheerfully, if we would be true disciples, and follow after the sad, worn Figure of the "Man of Sorrows." There are large and there are small crosses, heavy and light, rough and smooth, rudely formed and delicately finished. There are crosses of pain, and of sickness, of poverty, and of bereavement, and of sorrow, and of loneliness. There is a cross of bitter disappointment in one deeply loved; and a cross of living among people who cannot understand or feel for you. There is a cross of bridling the tongue and subduing the passions; of being useless to anybody; of sacrificing happiness for the sake of another; a cross in everything pure and good that the natural man must do or bear, laid upon us by the Master for our discipline and purification. But we fret under them, think them too hard or too heavy, grow weak and weary, and at last, perhaps, cast them aside. Christ has many followers of this sort. He has many lovers of His heavenly Kingdom, but few bearers of His Cross. He has many disciples who are desirous of consolation, but few of tribulation. He has many companions of His Table, but few of His abstinence. All desire to rejoice with Him; few are willing to endure anything for Him. Many follow Him to the breaking of Bread, but few to the drinking of the cup of His Passion. Many reverence His Miracles; few follow the ignominy of His Cross. Many love Him so long as no adversity befalls them; many bless and praise Him so long as they receive any consolation from Him; but if He hide Himself, or leave them for a little while, they fall either into complaining or carelessness, or backsliding and indifference.

For our good let us think of only one thing that is often a heavy cross to us—going to Church. Often there steals into our hearts the thought or the wish to stay at home from Church when we might go if we cared enough about it. We think we cannot go. We are all worn out, and tired, and sore. It is impossible to spend one hour in church; to watch with Christ one hour around His Altar; to devote one hour to earnest prayer and anxious thought. We are, O! so tired. Don't you think Christ was tired when He bore that Cross, and your sins, up the stony path leading to the top of Calvary? Don't you think He felt weary, and sore, and oppressed with the load your iniquities laid upon Him? The sweat of His Face, the thorn-pierced Brow, the scourged Back, the lacerated Hands and Feet, all suffered for our deliverance from sin, show the anguish of His Soul. Yet—with shame be it said—we are often too tired, nay, too unwilling, to bear one cross for Him, to spend one brief hour with Christ in the common prayers and praises of His Church.

Not only so, but some of us can spend all day Saturday, in the heat of summer, on a picnic, ending up in the evening with a dance. We run, and jump, and shout, and laugh, and play all day, without a thought of weariness. The whole thing is a pleasure to us, and we have what we call "a good time." We return home late at night sorry that it is all over, and hoping soon to go to another picnic or dance. The next morning is Sunday, the Lord's Day, the Day for Worship. But we feel too tired to go to Church; or it is too hot to go; or we find all sorts of other excuses to keep from going.

So one man prefers to read the Sunday papers, another takes a drive into the country; another swings in a hammock or sleeps away the blessed hours; or we must look after that Sunday dinner—most important that we should, our god being our belly, you know; or one thing or another may tempt us, and we consider ourselves fortunate in being thus tempted, for we do not care to go to Church anyhow, and prefer to stay at home. The simple truth of the matter is, "the flesh lusteth against the spirit and the spirit against the flesh," and "the carnal mind is enmity against God;" and so there is too much "flesh," too much "carnal mind," too much "natural man" in many who profess to be disciples and followers of Christ.

He who bade us take our crosses and follow, also said: "My yoke is easy and My burden light." He also said: "Ye shall not be tempted above that ye are able to bear;" for "My grace is sufficient for thee." If we grow weary under our crosses, can it be because we have not given us sufficient grace? Hardly that. But rather, because we do not use God's grace in bearing the temptation, but fall into the temptation without a struggle against it or a thought of its sinfulness. We follow, indeed, as He bids us; but at too great a distance. We come after Him, but with a faltering, halting step, and a weak, impatient heart. Let us bear our crosses for Him as He bore His for us—meekly, patiently, willingly; though it be too heavy to bear, like His; or the way be a way of sorrows, like His; or the path be marked with blood stains, as was His; or it lead to death, as did His. For beyond the cross lies the crown; and, as the chrysalis is changed into the beautiful butterfly, so this life with its many crosses, all its trials and sufferings, will at last unfold into a life of unending bliss, if we follow after Him in true discipleship—if we stay close by Him, faithful and devoted to the end.

THIRTY-SIXTH DAY OF LENT.

The Sorrow.

My Soul is exceeding sorrowful even unto death.—S. Matthew xxvi. 38.

Is it nothing to you, all ye that pass by? Behold, and see if there be any sorrow like unto My sorrow.—Lamentations i. 12.

THE book of Lamentations is the most sorrowful of all books. It is one great cry of agony. It is as if "every letter was written with a tear," as if every word had "the sound of a broken heart." The words are said of Jerusalem, and the City is the speaker. She hath grievously sinned; wherefore the Lord hath afflicted her in the days of His fierce anger, and she mourns her wretched state. All that once honored her despise her, and laugh her to scorn. Everywhere she sees nothing but the mocking arrows, the scornful lip, and the sidelong glance. She hears nothing but the brutal laugh and the coarse word. And as she buries her face in her hands to hide her shame, the cry goes forth from her heart and lip: "Is it nothing to you, all ye that pass by? Behold, and see if there be any sorrow like unto My sorrow."

But we turn from the sorrowing and lamenting City, suffering for her sins and suffering in the depth of utter loneliness, to that sorrowful scene of which the City is a type,—that most wonderful of all scenes, the "Man of Sorrows" lamenting for the sins of His people in the very shadow of His Cross.

Looking through the gloom of the Lenten Fast, our eyes meet those of One whose Face is wet with the hot and bitter tears of suffering; whose "visage so marred more than any man," shows the anguish wrung from His Soul by the sins of the whole world; whose pale Face shows, in every scar and every line, that, by reason of the iniquity of us all, He was indeed "a Man of sorrows, and acquainted with grief." Sorrow trespassed upon His cradle when, hunted by a murderous king, He was driven into Egypt. Sorrow followed His footsteps all through life. And now He too, as the City of old, sees nothing but the mocking crowd, and hears nothing but the coarse word and the brutal laugh; and from His trembling Lips comes the same pitiful and desolate cry: "Is it nothing to you, all ye that pass by? Behold, and see if there be any sorrow like unto My sorrow."

Ever since the Crucifixion of our Lord, has the Church tried to realize His sufferings. Especially in the Lenten Fast does the Church try to sympathize with Him in His temptation and sorrow and utter loneliness and gloom. The Church, by the Scriptures which she appoints to be read, takes us with our Lord into the wilderness to be tempted, into the depth of His humiliation, into the Upper Chamber, into dark Gethsemane, and then to the Cross. She makes us see the agony in the Garden, His bloody sweat, the betrayal, the scourging and buffeting, the crowning with thorns, the drinking of gall and vinegar, the driving of sharp nails into His Flesh, and the terrible suffering of the last hours of His Life. She makes us listen to Christ's predictions and warnings, to His prayers for His Apostles, to the groans and prayers in the Garden, to the formal accusation and the sentence of condemnation, the hollow mockery and brutal laughter, and the groans of His Passion. She makes us "behold the Man" in all His sorrow, and suffering, and desolation, and forsakenness. And we are then asked, yea, He Himself asks us, Are these—all these—nothing?—are they nothing to you? Do we behold with the tearful eyes of the Apostles and disciples, or with the unbelieving and merciless spirit of the mob which clamored for His death? Do we look upon Him face to Face, with the eye of faith, or with careless indifference? Have we that true, true love that speaks with Him heart to Heart and soul to Soul, or that hatred and that persecuting spirit of the Pharisees and priests, that urged on the mob into frenzy and murderous madness? Are these nothing to you?

"Behold, and see if there be any sorrow like unto My sorrow." See the greatness of His sorrow and suffering. "My Soul is exceeding sorrowful, even unto death." From His birth to His death, from the manger to the Cross, sorrow was the very hand-maid of the Son of God. He was born in a grotto-chamber, without any of the comforts of life, but with every indication of poverty and privation. A helpless Infant, a knife was uplifted for His slaughter, and He was hurried off by night into a foreign country to escape the blood-thirsty menaces of the king. Hungry and thirsty by day, he was homeless and shelterless by night. He had to look into the mouth of a fish for the money to pay His tax; and slept on the hillside beneath the clear blue sky because He "had not where to lay His Head." In privation and want, in suffering and bitterness, He trod the path of humiliation, knowing that it led to the Cross. This sorrow and suffering was rendered all the more acute by His contact with sin. What could have produced in His pure and perfect Soul, a more unutterable agony, than the exposure of the Essence of the Divine Life to all the wrongs, viciousness, baseness and degradation, moral and physical, all that is sensual, sordid, and selfish, mean, impure, and wicked, in man's heart; and to be exposed to this day by day, month by month and year by year? What could have wrung from His Lips more sharply that cry of pain and anguish, or what could have caused those bitter tears to flow more copiously, than the contact of His sinless Life with the sin of the whole world? Little is our sorrow compared with His; and little do we know of all, yea, of any of the sufferings and the sorrows of His Life. How can we, to whom sin is second nature, experience what it is for sinlessness to be exposed to everything that is sinful and antagonistic? We can, indeed, behold and see if any sorrow was ever like unto His sorrow; but there the measure of our life with His must end. Sympathy and pity must be turned into awe and adoration. More than that we cannot experience. Yet, great as His sorrow was—too great for our comprehension—is it nothing at all to us?—"is it nothing to you?" O! that we should have listless ears when that pitiful cry comes to us; that we should have eyes blinded by the world when we come in sight of that saddest of all scenes, that most sorrowful of all; that our faces should be turned away from our suffering Saviour when He appeals to us and says: "Is it nothing to you—to you—all ye that pass by!"

There was another aspect of His sorrow which we must notice. It was great, but it was also utterly desolate. Was ever any man on earth so lonely as He? "He trod the wine-press alone." "Behold, the hour cometh, yea, is now come, that ye shall be scattered every man to his own, and shall leave Me alone." He added, indeed, "yet, I am not alone, because the Father is with Me." But there came an hour when the Father also veiled His Face from "the Man of Sorrows," and drew the shadow of perfect isolation across the Saviour's soul; an hour when He felt Himself forsaken not alone by His disciples, but even by God; an hour when He saw not only the disciples pass out one by one and leave Him to His fate, but when He cried: "My God, My God, why hast Thou forsaken Me?" What a sense of desolate loneliness that must have been! "First the scrupulous Pharisees took the alarm; then the Sadducees; then the political party of the Herodians; and then the people;"* and when He came to His own for sympathy, they had "scattered every man to his own." "One denied Him; another betrayed Him; all deserted Him;" the Father also forsook Him. Could isolation have been more complete? Could loneliness have been more perfect? There, in the hands of His enemies, who thirsted for His blood; exposed to insult and mockery, and scourging and scorn; in the depth of humiliation and the bitterness of suffering, He was left alone.

All that great sorrow and desolate loneliness was caused by sin — by our sin — by your sins and mine;

---

* Giles.

and it was endured for our redemption from sin. When thinking of the Cross, we too often forget the sins of the world that the Cross atoned for; we are too apt to forget that it was our sins that He made His own, our sins that He carried to the Cross, our sins that shed His innocent Blood on Calvary, our sins that gave Him that sorrow and suffering. Did we think more of this, did we realize it more fully, the tremendous significance of the Cross would not only force itself upon us, but the Cross would possess for us far greater and lovelier attractions than anything on earth. We would see, as never before, something of that infinite Love it sets before us, of the nobility of that Love which could offer up its best and dearest for us—even the only-begotten Son of the Father. We should never be ashamed of the Cross, on which the Prince of Glory died, the Church's banner and the emblem of her Faith. And "we should keep ever fresh upon our brows the print of that same emblem received in Holy Baptism," and realize that we are "crucified with Christ." And that Cross—emblem of Christ's sorrow and suffering—should call forth in us more earnest devotion, more fervent zeal, and more steadfast faith. Did we think of our sins more than we do, the cry of our Saviour would not be uttered in vain; but we would desire to come nearer to Him, and, seeing the depth of His Heart, we would yearn to rise above the world and away from all sin, and to be folded in the embrace of His Everlasting Arms. Then would we repent us of our sins and be filled with love for such a loving, suffering Saviour—a love that should express itself in firm faith and perfect obedience all the days of our life.

THIRTY-SEVENTH DAY OF LENT.

The Desolation.

My God, My God, look upon Me, why hast Thou forsaken Me; and art so far from My health, and from the words of My complaint?—Psalm xxii. 1.

WE may know something of the inner depth of our Lord's Passion by thinking of that sense of loneliness and desolation that came over Him as time went on, a desolate loneliness which, however, we are unable to comprehend.

But was He, though much with men, yet not always lonely? Cloudy and dark was His whole life, cruel in its loneliness, complete in its solitude. He was born in a strange place, and unexpected by the multitudes around. In His Infancy He had to flee from the murderous knife of the king. His earthly parents understood not His mysterious Life, "nor understood they the saying which He spake unto them." In all that multitude which He mysteriously fed, what soul was there that sympathized with Him, or comprehended the meaning of His act? Often they sought to stone Him; often they took counsel how they might kill Him. Never once did they give Him that love which He so bountifully gave them. Though "He came unto His own, His own received Him not." His own city would have cast Him headlong from the hill-top. When the darkness deepened around His life, one of His own Apostles betrayed Him. When He was arraigned in the High Priest's palace, one of His own Apostles denied Him with oaths and curses, saying, "I know not this man of whom ye speak." All who for three years had been His constant companions and intimate friends, "forsook Him and fled."

Twice did the sense of deepening darkness, the feeling of increasing solitude, especially overshadow Him. Once in Gethsemane. But a few days before, by the tomb of His friend Lazarus, He prayed: "Father, I thank Thee that Thou hast heard Me, and I know that Thou hearest Me always." But when now in Gethsemane He prays: "If it be possible, let this cup pass from Me;" the cup will not pass away, and the Father seems not to hear. Strange and wonderful revelation is this. God the Father does not hear His Son; does not remove this bitterness from His Soul. His Ear, that was always open to the deep sighing of the sorrowful; that has always listened to the prayers of the Son of God, is deaf, and the Son must drink all the bitterness in that cup and empty it to the bottom. "When He looked for good, then evil came unto Him; and when He waited for light, then came darkness," a darkness that was overwhelming with terrors and affliction. His very Soul is poured out in that prayer, yet God doth not hear Him; His very Life is dissolved into a "bloody sweat," yet God doth not regard Him. He looked to the Lord for help, but the Lord hid His Face from Him and was silent. Oh, the intense loneliness of that hour!—the isolation, the solitude of that hour!

Again, on the Cross, was His Soul overcome with the sense of desolate loneliness. It was the strangest, "the darkest hour that ever dawned on sinful earth;"

and there was a profound, mysterious silence. Even the blood-stained mob had forgotten their fierce anger, and waited in breathless astonishment. The heavens were shaking on their foundations, and the very God and Father, if we dare suppose it, feared and trembled for His Son. The pallor of Death was creeping over His Face, when suddenly, from His parched Lips were forced those loud, awful, startling words — terrible the voice and still more terrible the words — "My God, My God, why hast Thou forsaken Me?" Can we believe it? Has the Son of God spoken truth? "Will the Lord absent Himself forever, and will He be no more entreated? Is His mercy clean gone forever, and is His promise come utterly to an end for evermore? Hath God forgotten to be gracious, and will He shut up His loving kindness in displeasure?" Oh, the blackness of those clouds that now drift over His Soul! — the overwhelming anguish that now, like an angry, mighty torrent, pours down upon His bruised and bleeding Form! Light has entirely left His Soul, and hope has, for a moment, left His Heart. Has God indeed deserted Him now? Has He indeed forsaken His Son? Has He indeed forgotten Him? Deserted — forsaken — forgotten! Oh, bitterest words of human suffering! Alone, and the powers of hell rage so fiercely. Alone, and the demons, with their fiery tongues, lick the foot of the Cross. Alone, and a myriad hellish hands are stretched forth to take and tear Him yet more cruelly. How Satan hounds on the spirits of evil in their fierce attack! How he laughs as he thinks that at last — at last — the Son of God is in his most merciless power, a helpless Victim! Alone, and forsaken — forsaken by His Father!

No; the sensible consolation of His Father's presence, the felt presence of the Trinity, had for one moment left Him. His sacred Humanity, for one moment at least, and to suffer the extremest limit of desolate woe, felt not the sustaining presence of Divinity in that crucified Form. But the Father was with the Son still, and led Him forth into "the valley of the shadow of death," and out again. It was only the overwhelming torrent of human sinfulness and misery pouring itself upon Him, that clouded for a moment the presence of Divinity, and forced from Him the cry of the forsaken. The weight of your sins and mine, the whole mass of the whole world's sin, lay upon Him; and the sorrow and the suffering which this gave Him were more than His weak human Frame could bear, or His Soul could endure. And so He felt desolate and forsaken of God as He had been forsaken of men.

And is this not hell itself? To be sunk into a flood of sin, to be surrounded, attacked, tormented by demons, to be deprived of the light of God's Countenance, what is this but a foretaste of outer darkness where there is weeping and gnashing of teeth—what is this but hell? And He endured this loneliness that we might never be alone. He went down into most utter desolation that no soul, not even yours or mine, should ever despair. Yea, that in all paths of our feverish life we might see His own footprints, and feel His sympathy and help. Out of the depths of this most bitter woe comes His love—that love which caused Him, which forced Him, to endure all this for our sakes. That help, that sympathy, that love, makes darkness light before us and crooked things straight. When storms beat upon us, and waves roll over our souls, we see above us the Form of the Son of God; and hear His voice saying unto us, as in the storm on Galilee: "It is I, be not afraid." Oh! the comfort, the consolation, the bliss, as we feel the warmth of that Love and find ourselves safe in the Everlasting Arms.

MAUNDY THURSDAY.

The Death.

He bowed His Head and gave up the ghost.—St. John xix. 30.

WHY rushes out this living mass of humanity from the city?—turbaned priests, the hoary seer, the Roman in his pride, the bridegroom and his bride, prince, beggar, soldier, Pharisee, old, young, bond and free, the lame, the blind, men, women, children, thousands, tens of thousands of the lower classes and the higher—and increasing in size as the minutes go by; rushing madly on, hither and thither, past each other and over each other, like dark clouds in a fierce storm, or like foaming waves in a tempestuous sea; and shouting, yelling, blaspheming? What means it all?

It is a glorious morn. The sun shoots higher and higher his warm, cheerful beams in the eastern sky. The Temple—minister of love and mercy—makes Mount Moriah appear more beautiful than ever before. The fields, far as the eye can reach, seem happy with their green spring covering. Yet, here, coming out of the city and ascending the hill towards Calvary, is a furious multitude crying for blood.

Still on comes the stream, out of the city, up the hill. But now we see in their midst One who is bowed down with grief, thorn-crowned, hand-cuffed, mangled and bleeding; and who seems to be the object of their taunts and curses, led on like a criminal and evidently sentenced to die the ignominious death of a slave. And through the tumult we hear the words: "Away with Him"—"Crucify Him." Who is He, and what has He done? Whom do they so rudely buffet and mock, and spurn? Behold in Him who is thus led as a malefactor to die the death of the Cross the Son of God and the Saviour of men.

The top of Mount Calvary is reached and the word of Death is given. He is bound to the Cross, His feet against the ledge at the bottom, His hands against the cross-piece at the top; and the long, sharp, cold, cruel nails are quickly driven into His quivering Flesh. With a mocking, scornful laugh, the Cross is raised with His body swinging upon it.

It is let fall with a thud into the hole dug for it. Oh, what agony in those hands and feet—what pain shoots through His whole body, as the heavy Cross comes down! The crowd cheers, the soldiers bow the knee in mocking homage, Scribes and Pharisees and priests exult. All clench their fists, gnash their teeth, and laugh and curse.

There stands the Cross, with its arms pointing upward and downward and to either side, as if in its muteness telling us of "the breadth and length and depth and height" of that "love of God" which "became obedient unto death, even the death of the Cross," that the sin of the world might be done away and man be "reconciled to God." The Saviour's arms opened wide thereon as if longing to take not only this pitiless mob but the whole world, yea, you and me, into His loving embrace, and draw us and all to His Heart.

Suffering, bleeding, dying, He bears the shame, the anguish of His Soul and the agony of His Body, without a murmur. No anger flashes from His Eye, no word of complaint, or of reproach, or of doom, escapes His Lips. He is meek, patient, good, and loving to the last. See how His wounds blacken, His Body writhes, and Heart heaves with pity and with agony! O, Almighty Sufferer, look down, look down from Thy triumphant infamy, from this Thy earthly Throne! Lo, He speaks—"Father, forgive them."—What, this cruel, wicked, bloody mob? Yes, "Father, forgive them," comes softly, sweetly from His feeble Lips. He inclines His Head to His sacred Bosom, and rests it upon His Father's Breast. Hark, He groans! See, He expires! "It is finished,"—all is finished; "His agony and bloody sweat," His "Cross and Passion," His Life, His Mission. The earth trembles, the sky darkens, The Temple rends, the rocks burst, the dead arise, the people are amazed and scatter in confusion. O, earth, earth, earth, darken thy form; O, sun, veil thy face because of this black and wicked deed! "Say to the mountains, fall on us; and to the hill scover us;" for the only hope of Israel, the only sure Deliverer is dead!

Yet, Mystery of mysteries! His Death was no loss to Israel, no end to all hope, no failure in that deliverance which He professed. He died, but it was through His Death that hope was to dawn upon Israel, and that deliverance should be made perfect. "Thus it behooved Christ to suffer," and to die. Thus was the ransom paid for our deliverance. Thus was the pledge given for our salvation. "I, if I be lifted up, will draw all men unto Me," said He. And here, and now, is He lifted up, as the serpent in the wilderness was lifted up; and, as all who looked upon the serpent lived, so here and now, all who look to the Son of Man and believe, shall be saved.

He died, and yet He lives; and we live in Him. He was removed from us, lifted up upon a higher and more enduring Throne than this His Cross; and yet He is ever with us. On that first Holy Thursday, in the "Upper Chamber," He instituted a Memorial of His broken Body and shed Blood, that all His disciples and servants might partake of Him and be filled. Calling His Omnipotence to aid His infinite Love for man, He concealed Himself in Bread and Wine; and ordained that, so long as a single drop of Adam's blood, sinful and sinning, shall flow upon earth, He should be held captive here, in this Sacramental means and Mystery Divine, and be ever present with us for our health and refreshment, while yet He is in glory at the right hand of God His Father.

In the Eucharistic Sacrifice, both He and we offer unto the Father,—He in intercession, we in sacred symbols, showing "the Lord's death till He come." In this Sacrifice He dies, as He died on the Cross; yet as on the Cross in the midst of death He still lived, so in this, in the very commemoration of His Death, He gives us His life. He not only gave His Life for us, but He gives it to us, and gives it in us; so that wholly and forever "He may dwell in us and we in Him." He dies and He lives; He dies once for all and lives forever,—lives in His Sacraments, in His Word, in His Ministry, in the hearts of His people. O, blessed Mystery! O, meritorious Death! O, perfect Life! God Himself hath appeared in the

Flesh, offered Himself an oblation for the sins of His people, atoned for them by shedding His own Blood, plead with God for them, and hath gone up into the true Sanctuary, "the heavenly place not made with hands," interceding for us by a continued presentation of His sacrificed humanity before the Father, openly in heaven, here veiled in Sacramental Mystery, till He hath "perfected for ever" all "them that are sanctified." Feeding on this mystery we live in Him and He manifests Himself to us, until, the veil drawn aside, we shall see Him "Face to face" and "know Him even as we are known" of Him.

GOOD FRIDAY.

The Passion.

My Heart is sore afraid within Me, and the terrors of death are fallen upon Me.—Psalm lv. 4.

WHAT in all the earth is so wonderful as a suffering God? Let us look upon this awful scene for a while; we did so yesterday, but with a view to the relation of His Death to His Holy Sacrament; let us now think, if we can, of the Death itself.

It is nine o'clock, Friday morning, the 7th of April, in the year 30 A. D. In obedience to the wild clamor of the people, Pilate, unwilling to offend them, surrenders the innocent Christ into their cruel and wicked hands. They have done their bloody work in the barracks of the Castle, have buffeted, scourged, mocked, spit upon, lashed, and insulted Him; and now the wild procession moves towards Calvary for the Crucifixion. We see them coming. In front is a centurion, the chief executioner. Then follows a soldier carrying a board on which is a peculiar inscription in the three civilized languages — Roman, Greek, and Hebrew. Next come four soldiers with hammer and nails; and between them a meek and lowly One whom we have often seen before, carrying, according to custom, the Cross on which He is to suffer. Then follow "two malefactors," each guarded by four soldiers, and each carrying his cross. And behind, a vast multitude, in wild confusion, pressing, and howling, and cursing, as they move along, and ever growing in numbers and becoming more clamorous as time flies.

Near by we see weeping women. What do they in such a crowd? Oh, mercy, Lord! They are Mary, the Mother of Jesus, and the other two Marys, and other women of Galilee, comforting with their presence and cheering with loving words the weary and wounded Son of Man and His Virgin Mother.

But the Cross is too heavy for His strength, already made weak by His long agony in the Garden, and by His bitter treatment at the hands of His enemies. See, He falls. Another takes it and bears it for Him. "Blessed are the merciful, for they shall obtain mercy;" and the mercy which the Cyrenian showed was no doubt blessed from heaven.

They come to Calvary and halt. The crowds press and surge around on all sides, and yell and blaspheme. "Away with Him!" "Crucify Him!" say they all. Why is He so patient and unresisting, who yet for three years past has shown Himself possessed with Divine power! Why does He not call forth from the heavens above that help which at all times was His, and which now could save Him to the uttermost! But His very weakness seems to say, "Lo, I came to do Thy will, O Lord;" and this—this is the will of God.

Watch their preparations. They are deliberate, yet their flashing eyes show a thirst for blood. They lay the Cross on the ground, pick up the Son of Mary, two at His Head and two at His Feet, and lay Him down upon it. With strong thongs they pinion His Arms and His Feet to it, shouting, and laughing, and blaspheming all the while. One picks up the hammer, the others the nails—a heavy hammer that can do deadly work, and long, sharp, cruel nails. Oh, that men can have hearts to do such work!—that men can be so cold, stony, and brutal, and wicked! The nail is held in position on one Hand, and the hammer swings high in mid-air. When it falls—Oh, merciful Father, why sparest not Thou Thy Son! It does fall, and but once, upon that nail on His Hand. Once is enough. It is driven through the quivering Flesh and into the wood. Now the hammer begins to beat measured strokes upon the nail, until it is firmly fixed on the arm of the Cross. Oh, the pain, and the suffering, and the torture, as the hammer falls and the nail sinks. Now might He have looked to His Father, and breathed the prayer of David, "O go not from Me, for trouble is hard at hand, and there is none to help Me."

But they have only begun their work. They drive a nail also into the other Hand, and into His crossed Feet; and with each blow of the hammer He suffers excruciating agony. His blood flows freely from the four wounds, and from the thorn-pierced Brow, and from His lacerated Back. The ground beneath Him is stained with His precious Blood, and still it is flowing from Him. They nail the board with its inscriptions at the head of the Cross, and raise it with its living—nay, its dying Mass swinging upon it. What pangs of torture rush through His Body as He feels His weight upon the nails! Sensitive to every pain—far more sensitive than most men are—He feels in every nerve of His Body the bitterness of His suffering. O God—"My God, why hast Thou forsaken Me, and art so far from My health, and from the words of My complaint? O, My God, I cry in the day time, but Thou hearest not. I am the very scorn of men, and the outcast of the people. All they that see Me laugh Me to scorn: they shoot out their lips, and shake their heads, saying, He trusted in God, that He would deliver Him: let Him deliver Him, if He will have Him." "They gape upon Me with their mouths. I am poured out like water, and all My Bones are out of joint. My strength is dried up like a potsherd. They pierced My Hands and My Feet; I may tell all My Bones." With curses on their lips, "they stand staring and looking upon Me." His enemies speak evil of Him and say, "He saved others, Himself He cannot save;" if He be the Son of God, as He says He is, "let Him come down from the Cross, and we will believe Him." They despised not only His pretensions and rejected His claims, but made Him a Man of sorrows, and loaded His Soul with grief. They maltreated Him; they reviled Him; they turned away their faces with sarcastic sneers. They esteemed Him not for His moral worth, nor for His endlessly forgiving and loving disposition, nor for His power over nature, and over disease, and over sin. Upon His unoffending Head fell the consequences, the curses, of our sins. They wounded— yea, pierced Him; they bruised—yea, crushed Him; and yet, here, on the Cross, as always, there was peace and there was love looking out of His Eye.

For three hours have they waited, and said, "When shall He die, and His Name perish?" Three long hours of horrible agony to our Lord. Weary of watching, and impatient, a soldier pierces His Side with a spear. Four wounds were not enough to satisfy this brutal mob. The inexpressible suffering which they caused Him was not enough to content them. Once more must they see His Body writhe in pain; and the spear furnishes the horrible spectacle. But He is too weak now to mind the thrust. His Blood is trickling, and His Life is fast ebbing away. His Eyes grow dim, as in the shadows of the evening hour. All the waves and storms go over His Soul, and still the enemy oppresses Him; but He minds them not now. At last His Head falls on His bosom, and His Soul wings its flight. With one great, long, loud, fierce, exultant shout, the mob disperses to the city and to their homes, leaving the body of their Saviour, and yours and mine, hanging in dim outline against that sudden and more than midnight darkness.

My friends, one word more. As we see Him hanging there, His sufferings ended and His sorrows over, let us learn that He sanctified suffering for us. Think what our sufferings would have been for our sins had He not suffered for us. Think of the agony which He has spared us by suffering it all Himself. And then how dare we turn against Him and crucify Him afresh by our misdeeds! How dare we refuse to love and serve Him who has thus loved and served us, and brought righteousness and redemption! Oh, let us from this day forth "walk worthy of the vocation wherewith we are called;" and then in every sorrow we shall see light, and every joy shall be a foretaste of heaven.

EASTER EVEN.

In Paradise.

There remaineth, therefore, a rest for the people of God.—Hebrews iv. 9.

AFTER many, many days of tossing on the waters of the flood, and being driven hither and thither by the angry winds, in darkness, the only object to be seen on the face of the earth, at length "the Ark rested." So our Lord, after a life of toil and suffering, especially in its latter end, when His Soul went out on the Cross, rested in peace on His Father's Breast.

All is "finished," as He said. Not only His Life, but His Work—the work the Father had given Him to do; not only the brutal treatment of His enemies, but His sorrows and sufferings, all are finished. "Messiah is cut off," "cut off out of the land of the living," "but not for Himself." Whither He went His enemies cannot come; cannot mock, buffet, spit upon, insult, bruise, scourge, smite Him; cannot crown Him with thorns, or pierce His Flesh with nails. All this is over, and ended forever. His weary Body lies in the peaceful rest of the tomb; His Soul is in the Paradise of God.

But what is Paradise? It is a garden of delight; Abraham's bosom; the vestibule of our "Father's house;" the blissful abode of all "departed spirits," who, dying in the Lord, looked forward to their "perfect consummation and bliss, both in body and soul, in eternal and everlasting glory." It is the park around the King's Palace, where the King loves to gather His people. It is the place where the dying thief met his Saviour, and where he now dwells with Him in the fuller glory and happiness of the saints in light.

More than this we know not. When we think of Paradise we seem to go entirely beyond our depth. It seems so vague and shadowy. It seems so distant, and wonderful, and mysterious, and dim, and vast, and strange. Yet thither our Saviour went, and there all who "desire to depart and to be with Christ" will meet Him. He is preparing some of those "mansions" for us. And when we get there it will not be so vague and shadowy as it now appears to our untaught minds to be, though it will still be vast and wonderful.

We look upon death with some degree of terror, and on the grave as a lonely place. But Christ did not find it lonely; neither shall we. Paradise has many grand sights and sounds; it has many blessed spirits whom we have loved here and lost awhile. To meet these and to be with them for ever; to talk with them again and to see their unbroken happiness; to feel again the warmth of their love, and be thrilled again by a touch of their hands, this, if this were all, would be enough for our everlasting happiness.

But this is not all. It has a glorious company of redeemed souls, gathered out of all lands. There is "the glorious company of the Apostles, the goodly fellowship of the Prophets, the noble army of Martyrs;" the holy men and women of the Old Testament and of the New; all the pious and saintly souls that have peopled the centuries, and who, like a mighty host, are gathered around the Throne and are singing the praises of "the Lamb that was slain." These all are in Paradise.

But better company than these will we meet there. There, in unapproachable Light, will be God our Father, who has loved and forgiven us; God the Son, who has redeemed us; God the Holy Ghost who Sanctifies us. God is everywhere; but He is here with especial fulness of glory, and we will see Him here in ever newer revelations of love and blessing. And this will be Paradise.

Into this abode, "this better country, that is an heavenly," our Saviour and the penitent thief went after death; and it was to them a place of rest. So it will be to us.

Think of the security of that rest. Here the holiest among us have temptations and trials, sorrows and anguish. They know not what a day may bring forth. Their "going out" may be unto suffering; and their "coming in" may be the last. Man "fleeth as it were a shadow, and never continueth in one stay." The life of the body and the life of the soul are alike tempted and pained. But in Paradise there will be no more temptation or suffering. The sense of security that will steal over the soul, as we wake up in the likeness of Christ, will be a thousand times intensified when we see Christ Himself by our side.

But think also of the happiness which comes with that rest—a happiness which comes with a clearer vision of God. "Now, we see through a glass darkly; but then, face to face. Now, we know in part; but then shall we know even as we are known." And, oh, the bliss of one brief glance at our Saviour's Face! To know that we are no longer in the dark valley, and need no longer His rod and His staff, but that now we are in safety "with Christ;" to feel the comforting assurance of His power; to have a blessed, restful confidence in His tender love; to hear His gracious words; to look upon His Face—His thorn-pierced Face—and see with our own eye the Love that redeemed us—surely there can be no bliss like this. And this is the bliss of Paradise.

Once more think that our Lord went into the rest of Paradise to secure it especially for us—for you and for me. It is our own. It awaits us at death. It awaits all those who are members of Him. In that day, when heaven and earth shall sink away, and a new heaven and a new earth shall come forth; when His elect are numbered; then, borne on His Bosom and tinctured with Holy Blood, we shall soar from this tranquil bower into the higher rest of the Heaven of heavens.

> " O Paradise, O Paradise,
>   Who doth not crave for rest?
> Who would not seek the happy land
>   Where they that loved are blest;
> Where loyal hearts, and true,
>   Stand ever in the light,
> All rapture, through and through,
>   In God's most holy sight?
>
> " Lord Jesus, King of Paradise,
>   O, keep us in Thy love,
> And guide us to that happy land
>   Of perfect rest above;
> Where loyal hearts, and true,
>   Stand ever in the light,
> All rapture, through and through,
>   In God's most holy sight."

www.ingramcontent.com/pod-product-compliance
Lightning Source LLC
Chambersburg PA
CBHW021825230426
43669CB00008B/870